The BROWNIE *Lover's* BIBLE

Over 100 Delicious Recipes

Lisa SLATER

whitecap

Edited by Elaine Jones
Revised edition edited by Grace Yaginuma
Proofread by Joan E. Templeton
Design by Mauve Pagé
Typesetting by Setareh Ashrafologhalai
Photography by Dominique and Cindy Duby
    and Christopher Freeland

Printed in China

**Library and Archives Canada Cataloguing
    in Publication**

Slater, Lisa
        The brownie lover's bible : over 100 delicious recipes / Lisa Slater.

Includes index.
Previously published under title: Brownie points.
ISBN 978-1-55285-939-1

        1. Brownies (Cookery). I. Title.

TX771.S55 2008   641.8'654   C2008-902128-2

The publisher acknowledges the financial support of the Government of Canada through the Book Publishing Industry Development Program (BPIDP) and the Province of British Columbia through the Book Publishing Tax Credit.

08 09 10 11 12 5 4 3 2 1

CONTENTS

THIS BOOK IS DEDICATED TO:

My parents, who are living proof that brownies promote longevity; my husband, Howard, who is living proof that brownies aren't fattening; and my children, Jo and Ali, who are living proof that brownies make you smart.

To all of you: thank you for your loving support throughout the creation of *The Brownie Lover's Bible*.

ACKNOWLEDGMENTS AND APPRECIATIONS

This would have been a solitary project if not for all the enthusiastic testers who fearlessly sampled every brownie, cookie and cake recipe. These include my colleagues at Whole Foods Market Toronto (whose passion for food is only surpassed by their passion for eating and critiquing what they eat, especially after a grueling eight hours of counting inventory), as well as my husband Howard's many students and teaching associates at Ryerson University. Thank you all for sacrificing your waistlines in pursuit of the perfect brownie recipe. Thank you too for your open and honest feedback when you discreetly tossed one of my less successful endeavors in the trash.

And then there are all those who worked on this book, notably Alison Maclean, who encouraged the project from the beginning. Editing a cookbook may seem like a dream job—all those recipes to try before anyone else. In fact, it has to be one of the most painstaking forms of editing there is. Others who pored over this manuscript: Elaine Jones, whom I only know thanks to the miracles of email; Marial Shea who pulled it all together, keeping me calm when I thought the whole project would melt like an underbaked brownie; and Grace Yaginuma for her eagle

eyes and consistent insistence on consistency, making this second edition better than ever. A special thanks to my colleague and friend Christine Vié for her proofreading in record time. Thanks too to Mauve Pagé for the bigger, better and bolder redesign of this edition, making it far easier to use.

And then there are a few family members who committed their time and attention to various parts of this book: my sister-in-law, Brenda, whose comments were both funny and perceptive, as well as my niece, Emma, who spent precious vacation days editing the final edition. Ladies, thank you, too.

Last but not least, are all the other members of my family, Abby, Morry, Maya, Ken, Simon, Eli, Michael, Kathy, Alexis, Nathaniel and Aaron, all of whom at one time or another encouraged the writing of these recipes through their enthusiastic consumption of my various brownie fantasies and then went out and bought the book for their friends. Unbeknownst to them, they were all part of a covert experiment to see if anyone, at any time, would turn down chocolate desserts. Despite diets and dietary restrictions that ran the gamut from kosher to cholesterol, from low carb to low fat, the results are in and not all that surprising: no one can resist a chocolate dessert, especially if it's a brownie.

The Evolution of *The Brownie Lover's Bible*

Brownies are what I call the little black dress of the baking trade: as perfect in a pan at the school fundraising sale as they are all dolled up on a plate and served after an elegant meal. Dress them up with a necklace of raspberries, or serve them no-frills, stacked one on top of the other for easy access. No matter how you present them, virtually everyone loves them . . . and for those few who don't, the recipes in this book should convince them of what they're missing! In fact, someone I know, my friend Sharon's husband, claimed he didn't like brownies until he tasted one of my recipes. Whole new vistas of chocolate were opened up to him.

Initially, I set out to develop over 50 brownie recipes, each one different and unique. And I was determined not to get too weird, because what's the point? How often are you going to bake Wasabi Brownies? Or Lemongrass Brownies? Sure, as a once-in-a-while showstopper you might, but I wanted recipes you would return to again and again—and more importantly, crave again and again.

It rapidly became difficult to create recipes that were distinctly different from one another and that fit into my original mandate: deep, dark and delicious. Over the years, in and out of my restaurants, I have perfected a few recipes that I adore: easy and fudgy and also versatile, meaning I don't always have to turn the batter into brownies.

Eventually, from using these wonderful batters, I have developed ways to re-create the richness of brownies in recipes as disparate as Brownie Curd (page 8) and Brownie Blobs (page 126). So now you'll find, in addition to many true brownie variations, recipes that aren't technically brownies but which will, nonetheless, deliver the intense chocolate flavor imparted by their muse, The Classic Brownie (page 29). Brownie Heaven, it turns out, can be found equally in a Peanut Butter Caramel Tart (page 184).

All of the recipes are simple, but some have detailed instructions. If you're making something for the first time, it's helpful to have more rather than less detail. Some of the recipes consist of several individual components that need to be made either ahead of time or one right after the other. But none demand a huge amount of prior baking experience.

The Introduction provides important information on ingredients and technique. Nobody has less time than professional bakers, so the section on *mise en place* will make your life very easy. This is how professional bakers work: components are made and at the ready.

Chapter One is also an introduction of sorts, providing recipes for components that make dessert assembly quick and easy. With these recipes on hand in the fridge or freezer, you'll be able to assemble desserts in minutes.

Chapter Two has the fudgiest, richest brownie recipes on the planet. These aren't your normal brownies. Virtually all of them have firm but melting edges and interiors that verge on the molten when warm. The Fudge Factor (page x) is a one to four scale indicating just how fudgy each recipe is. Once at room temperature or chilled, the brownies firm up to an amazing, chewy, not overly sweet, fudgy consistency. Served with a dollop of vanilla ice cream, they're the best dessert there is. Period.

The last few chapters of the book use chocolate to create the soul-satisfying quality of brownies in puddings, cookies, cakes and tarts.

So what are you waiting for? Turn the page and get going! Don't forget to have fun and share the results with your friends, who will think you are a baking genius. But most of all, enjoy!

Brownie (and Other Baking) Basics

What's good for the goose is good for the gander, as the familiar saying goes. In this case, you could say what's good for brownies is good for baking in general. Basic brownies are just the first stepping stone to more complex recipes. Master these techniques and approaches to ingredients and you're on your way to being a competent and calm home baker. Remember, learning how to bake is fun: it allows you to concentrate on something other than work—or whatever's bothering you. At the end of it all, you will have something delicious to show for your efforts, and best of all you will have gained confidence to do more.

Ingredients

These days, cookbooks go into great detail about required ingredients. The beauty of brownies, and the recipes inspired by them, is that they don't ask for much: fresh unsalted butter, fresh and/or organic large eggs and good-quality chocolate. Granulated white and light or dark brown sugar. Pure vanilla, no artificial flavors or colors. Fresh nuts, almost always lightly toasted and cooled before chopping. (I toast entire bags' worth and keep them double-bagged in my freezer to save time in recipes.) Whipping cream with a minimum 35% butterfat and not ultrapasteurized, because the flavor of pasteurized cream isn't nearly as good as old-fashioned whipping cream and it takes forever to whip. Seasonal—and even better, local—fruit because it tastes better and is cheaper. Kosher salt because it brings out the flavor of chocolate like nothing else. (There are times when I sprinkle salt on top of my brownies for the most intense chocolate experience ever. Go ahead, try it! You'll be amazed at the difference in taste.)

And then there's flour. I use unbleached flour (or, for pâte sucrée, regular pastry flour) as well as instant blend flour, the latter because it blends without lumps in a sticky batter, and the former simply because I prefer it. Instant blend flour is available in your grocery's baking section as "Wondra."

Lately, though, I have started to use more whole grains in my baking without any loss of quality. Try to find stone-ground whole wheat flour if you can, and keep it refrigerated or frozen so it doesn't go stale. For brownie recipes, I use the same amount of whole wheat flour per white flour, except that I use 1 tablespoon (8 g) less.

Chocolate

There's so much great-quality chocolate on the market that I won't recommend one over another, except to say that Scharffen Berger 99% unsweetened chocolate is the best in its class, and is all I use, because of its superior flavor. Still, you can use any supermarket unsweetened chocolate as a replacement, but check the label before you buy your chocolate and don't buy anything that has sugar as the first ingredient, or that includes the artificial vanilla, *vanillin* (not only because it doesn't taste good but because no one knows how to pronounce it properly). Scharffen Berger, Ghirardelli, Callebaut, Schokinag, Lindt, Valrhona—these are all chocolates that work well in my recipes as long as you use unsweetened, bittersweet or milk chocolate, as specified.

There are a lot of varietal chocolates available these days too. Just like varietal wines and coffees, they are made from one kind of cocoa bean or another and originate from a single country of origin. They tend to be very expensive and vary greatly in taste and quality.

My advice is to taste them first to decide if the price delivers something extraordinary.

Most of the time, I use bittersweet chocolate with a 64% to 70% cocoa content. The higher the cocoa percentage and the cocoa butter content, the richer the taste, but you'll have to make some recipe adjustments. Should you find yourself with only a 70% or higher chocolate and in desperate need of making one of the recipes calling for a lower percentage, adjust your sugar upwards a bit and your butter down to take into account the higher cocoa butter content in some of these intense chocolates. Brownies are incredibly sturdy and won't wilt with recipe tinkering, although they may ooze and become a bit greasy while baking, or never completely firm up until refrigerated, so that you may not get what you expected. But 99% of the time, you get something delectable, even if it wasn't exactly what you anticipated. (For the best discussion yet on the characteristics and performance of various kinds of chocolate, read Alice Medrich's book *Bittersweet*.)

Cocoa now comes in a variety of forms too. The only thing you need to know for this book is that any cocoa will do. Look for the darkest cocoa you can find and stay away from light-colored ones, which won't deliver you the rich complexity provided by darker ones. (Note that using Dutch-processed cocoa won't make much of a difference in most of the recipes in this book. The alkali in this kind of cocoa counteracts the acidic flavor of leavening agents, but most of these recipes don't call for any baking soda or baking powder. And actually, this acidity isn't that unpleasant at all.)

As a hasty baker, I'm always looking for shortcuts. Melting chocolate, however, isn't one of the places where one should try to speed things up. Chocolate burns easily if set directly over heat, so my preferred methods are as follows. While you can melt chocolate in the microwave, I find it more effort than it's worth because the chocolate can easily burn and requires constant attention. My advice? Stick to the stovetop method. Over low heat, bring about 1 inch (2.5 cm) of water to a simmer in a sauté pan. You'll need a deep bowl that is smaller than the pan's diameter so that it doesn't touch the sides, leaving about an inch (2.5 cm) all around. Stainless steel works the fastest. Place chopped chocolate in the bowl (yes, a pain, but in the end worth it in the reduction of melting time), and place the bowl directly in the water and on the bottom of the sauté pan. Watch carefully. When most of the chocolate has melted, remove the bowl from the pan and stir, allowing the residual heat to do the rest of the work.

You can also set a bowl resting snugly in a saucepan of simmering water, but I prefer the above method as it's simple and doesn't risk water from suddenly escaping steam getting into your chocolate.

Under no circumstances should you allow any water or steam to come into contact with melted chocolate. It will "seize," which means it will clump up and become totally unusable. Don't even think about using it again. Throw it out and start over.

Many brownie recipes call for melting butter and unsweetened chocolate together as a first step and then adding sugar and eggs. If the mixture of butter and chocolate is too hot, the fat may separate from the chocolate, leaving a shiny film on top. In this case, like making mayonnaise, you need to reincorporate the fat (also known as emulsifying) back into the other ingredients. This is best achieved through rapid whisking and/or cooling. Or, try whisking in a small amount (1 Tbsp/15 mL) of chopped chocolate to bring down the temperature. Don't add your eggs unless the chocolate and butter look thick and glossy and fully incorporated.

Equipment

Brownies are wonderfully versatile from the standpoint of equipment: round, square and rectangular pans all work, as do tart tins, muffin cups, pie pans, even espresso cups. In these recipes, you can use an 8-inch (20 cm) square, a 9-inch (23 cm) square, a 9- × 13-inch (23 × 33 cm) or a 10-inch (25 cm) round pan.

For the most part, I've chosen three pan sizes for my brownies. This doesn't mean that you can't make them in a round pan or even a smaller or larger pan, it just means that you'll have to adjust baking times because you'll either get a thicker or thinner brownie. My recipes for brownies tend to be large, and while you may certainly bake them off all at once, you don't have to do so, since the batter refrigerates and freezes wonderfully for months. As for the number of brownies in each recipe, that depends: brownies like these are very rich; therefore, a little goes a long way. In the recommended 9-inch (23 cm) square pan, you could get as few as 9 or as many as 25! It all depends upon what you want to use them for: the main attraction or supporting role.

Always line your pans with a single piece of parchment paper, wide enough to cover the bottom and long enough to hang over parallel sides of the pan. This way you can grip the parchment sides so you can lift out the finished brownie slab. Remember, too, to grease the exposed sides of the pan with vegetable spray. Always allow the brownies to cool completely before lifting them out of the pan.

Run a knife around the edges and they should come up easily. If you have opted not to use parchment paper, the brownie slab may stick to the pan, especially if it's been chilled. In this case, set the pan over low heat on your stovetop, moving it from side to side for about 20 seconds, and the brownie slab will lift right out.

Many nonstick cookie sheets are just that, and won't need either paper liner or spray, but if you don't have nonstick sheets, I urge you to get yourself a roll of parchment paper. Don't throw it away after every use. Just wipe it clean, let it dry, and set it flat in a drawer until you bake again. Silpat or other pan liners are also good. Although expensive, the liners last virtually forever and are well worth the investment.

Baking

Since many of these recipes may make more brownie batter than you need, fill your pans three-quarters of the way to the top, storing what is left over in the fridge or the freezer. Brownie batter is almost indestructible and has a long shelf life, thanks to the high proportion of sugar and fat, both preservatives. I have never had brownie batter go moldy. I put the batter in a lidded container and cover the surface of the batter with some plastic wrap as a double form of protection from air and moisture.

There's no need to adjust your baking times or temperatures unless you've poured the batter far deeper than usual. In that case, simply add time in the form of 5-minute increments until you see the telltale signs of brownie perfection: risen sides, barely firm but not liquid center, a few cracks. It's always better to err on the side of underbaking brownies rather than overbaking them. If the times don't work for you as directed in the recipes, make sure your oven is working at the designated temperature by using an oven thermometer, or adjust the times to reflect whether your oven is too hot (reduce the heat and lower the rack) or too cold (increase the heat, raise the rack). No matter what, don't leave your baking, at least the first time you make a recipe, to chance. Keep an eye on the baking pan by looking at it through the oven window, and once in a while, open the door and jiggle the pan to see how it's coming along. It's not a cake or a soufflé where sudden moves may wreck the whopping 10 minutes it took you to put it together! And notice what your kitchen smells like as the brownies are baking—generally, if you can smell something wonderful, they tend to be ready, so check on them as soon as you notice a chocolate aroma wafting through the air.

Baking is an exact art when it comes to the chemistry of ingredients but it can be inexact in the timing of the actual baking. Fluctuating humidity can affect baking times, as can the color of your pans and your oven temperature. What's more, your expectation of the recipe outcome may not be what the author intended.

What is commonly thought of as a brownie is definitely not what I intend in my recipes. *My brownies are intended to be fudgy rather than cakey.* However, the beauty of my recipes is that they're flexible. If you prefer them less fudgy, just bake them a few more minutes. At the same time, you have to exercise some judgment when you make any recipe for the first time: is the outcome to your liking and, if not, what can you do to get it where you want it? With some recipes, it's simply not possible, but happily, in most of these brownie recipes (not so much for other recipes), you can adjust baking times to affect outcome. Just be aware that the more you heat chocolate, the more chocolate flavor you lose because the compounds that create chocolate's flavor are highly volatile when heated.

Use all your senses to determine doneness. If your kitchen has an intoxicating smell of chocolate, you know the brownies should be ready soon. If a toothpick put into the center comes out covered with liquid batter, you know it has a way to go, but if it comes out with really thick batter on it, then it's all but ready. (If there's nothing at all, it's possible that it's been overbaked.) The edges will be firm and the center will be slightly puffed but jiggly without being liquid underneath the surface. You will probably see shallow cracks too on top. Watch the stages of baking as they occur: the top first gets shiny, then begins to look puffy and matte with the feel of liquid batter underneath when you tap it. Halfway through baking, the edges will be firm, the center will start to rise and even crack a little, but underneath will be jellylike.

When you remove the brownies from the oven, the center will fall, creating the luscious denseness these brownies are famous for. As they cool, the brownies continue to bake and the center firms up. If you slice them a half hour out of the oven, most of the fudgier brownies will have a range of brownie textures within the pan: the edges will slice well and hold their shape while the center pieces may actually ooze a little bit. If this is too gooey for you, just increase the baking time by 5-minute increments until you reach the texture you prefer, being aware that for the center to be firm, the edges will be firmer still. Or, follow my instructions and let the brownies cool completely to room temperature and/or refrigerate them, at which point the center will no longer be oozy, but it will certainly be fudgy. With my recipes, you won't get cakey brownies no matter how long you bake them! There are recipes for chocolate cakes with a deep brownie taste that you can bake into squares, but these are not, to my mind, true brownies.

In the end, these recipes are for you and what you like so don't be afraid to experiment. There's really not much you can do to ruin most of them unless you burn them—in which case, I'd say you've probably overbaked them!

Fudge Factor

To convey the difference between my brownies and more traditional ones, I've created a Fudge Factor scale of one to four (see page 25). The ratings next to each recipe tell you how comparatively moist and fudgy each brownie will be. The Classic Brownie (page 29) and Bar None Brownies (page 34) stand as paragons of brownie fudginess. All else is rated against them. At room temperature, edges will be slightly crisp but towards the center of the slab, the brownie will be increasingly soft to the touch, verging on molten. Chilled, the center will firm up and be dense with chocolate without the overwhelming sweetness of fudge. At no time will these brownies be cakey or have much of a crumb. They're stubbornly rich and decadent and proud of it.

Storage

Among the many attributes that make brownies wonderful, ease and length of storage are foremost.

Virtually all the recipes in this book have longer storage potential than regular baked goods. In general, consume recipes that contain fruit (fresh or frozen) the same day they're made. Those without fruit can frequently be refrigerated and frozen with little, if any, loss in quality. Just make sure you wrap everything first in plastic and then in foil. Put soft and sticky items, like cheesecake brownies, on a cardboard base and then wrap them. Don't forget to identify and date them since your freezer will quickly fill up with foil packages of various shapes and sizes; you think you'll remember what's in them a week later, but I promise you, they will all look alarmingly the same. Having a well-stocked freezer with well-identified items is a sign that you're on your way to being a great pastry chef, with fully prepared and partially completed items ready to finish at a moment's notice.

Keeping brownies in the fridge intensifies their fudge-like qualities. However, cold masks their deep, rich flavor, so serving them slightly warm might sacrifice texture but definitely enhances flavor. Fifteen to 20 seconds in the microwave is enough to warm up a brownie perfectly.

Weights and Measures

When I was a kid, there was this puzzle: Which weighs more, a pound of feathers or a pound of lead? Most of us would choose lead until we realized that a pound is a pound whether it's made of feathers, lead or chocolate. How much space (volume) one pound of lead would take up, compared to a pound of feathers, is another story. And would that pound of feathers always take up the same amount of room or slightly more or less depending upon how fluffy it was?

All this is to explain why professional cooks use weight as the preferred method of portioning their ingredients. Time after time, 180 g or 10 oz (by weight) of cocoa is the same whether it's packed, tamped, sifted or scooped, whereas a cup (by volume) of cocoa is a good 10 to 15 g

Ingredient	Measure	Grams	Ounces
Granulated sugar	1 cup (250 mL)	200	7
Brown sugar, medium packed	1 cup (250 mL)	220	8
Icing sugar	1 cup (250 mL)	120	4 1/4
All-purpose flour	1 cup (250 mL)	130	4 1/2
Whole wheat flour	1 cup (250 mL)	130	4 1/2
Chocolate, average chip-sized pieces	1 cup (250 mL)	175	6 1/4
Raisins	1 cup (250 mL)	120	4 1/4
Butter	1 cup (250 mL)	227	8
Peanut butter	1 cup (250 mL)	227	8
Whole nuts (average)	1 cup (250 mL)	120	4 1/4
Eggs, large	1 each	50	1 3/4

(almost ½ oz) less if it's sifted versus scooped. The same goes for flour, a critical ingredient in most of these recipes.

Variations in flour weight can affect the outcome so the result is never the same—sometimes too dense, other times not dense enough. The key is not only to have a good recipe, but also to weigh ingredients rather than measure them so you have similar results time after time. Home scales are now readily available, and I urge you to get one before considering any other new gadget for your kitchen. Of course it's also useful, if, after making and eating all these brownies, you find yourself on a diet and needing to portion your meals . . . but let's not go there!

This is also why recipes differentiate between such things as "1 cup nuts, chopped" and "1 cup chopped nuts." The first asks you to measure your nuts then chop them. The second, to chop some nuts and then measure. Chopped nuts take up less room than nut pieces so you can

get a lot more into a cup. Therefore, 1 cup chopped nuts will weigh differently than the same *volume* of whole nuts.

When you make a recipe a second time, it will be difficult (but not impossible) to duplicate exactly what you did the first time unless you weigh ingredients. Despite this, most cookbooks call for volumetric measures, such as cups or milliliters. This works fine, most of the time, but if you want consistency, invest in a kitchen scale (digital if possible) and you'll never look back. You'll soon become acquainted with the conversion of volume measures to their weight equivalents. Furthermore, you'll be surprised at how inaccurate measuring cups and spoons can be. I have different styles of measuring cups and spoons and each one holds a different amount of sugar, so it's no wonder my baking results varied until I converted to weighing ingredients. Keep in mind, though, that it's difficult to weigh small amounts, which is why anything from about 2 Tbsp (30 mL) and under is given by volume here.

"The metric system." Say these words to most Americans and they cringe. As someone who grew up with ounces and pounds, and who came to Canada just as the metric system was mandated into law, I can tell you it's so much easier to use than the Imperial system. Based on 1,000 g to a kilo, which is equivalent to 1 liter of water or 1,000 mL, everything else just falls into place. Think of a pound of butter as slightly less (454 g) than half a kilo; think of the 5 cups of sugar (200 g each) that make a kilo and you'll be able to determine whether that 5-pound (2.25 kg) bag of sugar holds enough for you to make two batches of brownies. Flour is a bit trickier: some pastry chefs use 140 g as their 1-cup equivalent, while I use 130 g. This doesn't matter too much if you adhere to the recipe as shown, but if you decide to expand the recipe by multiplying it tenfold, then that minor 10 g difference can be the difference between the recipe being faithful to the original or becoming something different and not altogether that pleasing. This is another reason to use weight as your preferred portioning method. When you decide that you need four times the recipe, you'll guarantee with 4 × 100 g that each time you'll get 400 g, not 379 g or 412 g.

For those who are still not convinced that metric (and weight) is a superior system, see the conversion chart on the previous page for some of the main ingredients in this book.

Perfect Bars Every Time: Slice Your Brownies Like a Pro

Have you ever wondered how bakery brownies are so perfectly cut? I did too until I worked in a bakery. There are two ways to do it.

The old-fashioned way is to measure very carefully with a ruler. First, we trimmed the edges, saving them for either rum balls or afternoon snacks. Then we scored the brownie slab at even intervals both vertically and horizontally. We dipped a BIG, sharp chef's knife in hot water and wiped it dry, then made a single slice from one end of the knife to the other. Because the brownie slab was bigger than the knife, it took a few slices. And because the brownie was sticky, after each slice we dipped the knife into hot water and wiped it again before the next slice. This would keep the edge of the brownies, especially iced ones, perfectly vertical and sharp.

One day, we got a nifty gadget that looked like an expanding child safety gate with wheels on the ends. We could expand or contract it to create the intervals we wanted, vertically and horizontally, and roll the wheels, which would score the brownies evenly. This saved an incredible amount of time and produced perfect brownies every time. Alas, these cutters are expensive for the home baker, so I suggest using the old-fashioned ruler and chef knife method. (However, if this accordion cutter intrigues you, it can be found at professional baking and restaurant supply stores.)

To slice professional-looking bars, invert the baked, chilled brownie slab onto a metal cooling rack. Place both rack and slab on a cookie sheet lined with parchment paper. Pour warm glaze (not hot—if it's too hot it will run off the sides and be absorbed by the brownie, which you don't want) over the center of the brownie slab until you have a pool that runs the width of the slab. Use an offset spatula to gently nudge or push the glaze down to, and over, the ends. You're not frosting the brownie slab but glazing it, so a gentle touch will keep the glaze shiny and smooth. If there's not enough glaze to make it to the ends, simply pour some more over the top. If you feel daring and the rack isn't too big, pick up both rack and brownie slab and tip it in the direction that you want the glaze to flow. Don't worry about using too much glaze. It will fall onto the parchment paper where you can scoop it up easily when it's cooled, strain it and place in a plastic container for future use. This isn't a time to skimp. Beautiful glazing requires lots of glaze to do the job. Place the glazed slab in the fridge to chill thoroughly, about 2 hours before cutting.

Run a sharp chef's knife under hot water to heat it, then dry thoroughly. Place the brownie slab on a cutting board. Remove the rough edges and measure the slab, scoring it at even intervals. Place the tip of the knife at one end and firmly cut down into the brownie. Draw the knife through the bar without bringing it up through the glaze. This will guarantee a straight edge. Remove the knife, run it under hot water and wipe it dry. Repeat with each cut. Your edges will be sharp and professional looking.

Brownie Offspring

A recent conversation with one of my editors, Alison, reminded me that most people, when they have a baking failure, simply discard the mess and start over or vow never to make that recipe again.

Alison was bemoaning the fact that a brownie recipe from a prominent chef's book didn't turn out and she had poured $15 worth of fancy chocolate into it. The problem was overcooked edges and a gooey center. "What did you do with it?" I asked. "I threw it out," she replied. I was

aghast. There's so much you can do with brownie batter that you should never throw it out unless you have burned it. (For that, there really is no cure.)

So, Alison, these tricks of the trade are for you. Professional chefs rarely throw anything out. Here are a few things to do with stale, overcooked or underdone brownies, brownies you thought were so-so but not up to snuff—or maybe you just made too damn many of them! And it happens to me, too. For example, for this new edition I wanted to fix a typo that had cropped up in one of the recipes. I forgot how it was originally written, so I experimented a little to fix it. BIG mistake. I ended up with something not very tasty. But did I throw it out? Never! I just turned it into a crumble topping by adding additional sugar, some melted butter and cinnamon. Voilà! It wasn't wasted.

MUSHY/GREASY BROWNIES

This is often the result of too little baking time, too much sugar or butter or substitution of a higher percentage chocolate, or omission of a key ingredient, like eggs (it happens).

Return the pan to the oven and bake another 5 to 10 minutes at 300°F (150°C). The edges might overcook but these can easily be trimmed. If this doesn't fix the problem, proceed to the next step.

Place the brownies in the fridge to see if they'll firm up. If so, eat them!

If refrigeration doesn't do the trick, and your brownies are still liquidy, place the whole mess in the mixing bowl of an electric mixer fitted with the paddle attachment. Beat the hell out of them, until you have a fairly smooth mixture. It won't be like new but it will have character! Add 1 or 2 eggs, and beat until smooth. Pour into a parchment-lined brownie pan and bake at 300°F (150°C) for 30 to 40 minutes. Or, pour into a cake pan, cover with foil, and place in a hot water bath and bake until firm, about an hour. You'll now have Brownie Pudding.

If you don't want to re-bake, soften a quart of ice cream and fold the brownie mixture into it. Voilà! You have created Brownie Ripple Ice Cream.

OVERBAKED BROWNIES

These tend to be dry, not the texture you were after. Often there's a 1-inch (2.5 cm) perimeter of tough, crisp crust, while the center of the brownie is great. Simply trim the edges and save them.

Use the trimmed edges or the whole mess of overbaked brownies to make Brownie Crumble Topping: Rub the brownies between your hands over a bowl to create rough, large crumbs. Place them on a cookie sheet and dry out in a 250°F (120°C) oven for about 20 minutes, tossing from time to time. Use them as is as a topping for fruit salads or ice cream or as garnish for desserts. Or, for a fruit crumble, moisten them with some melted butter and plop them on top of your fruit; or use them to make Brownie Triscotti (page 134).

Brownie crumble makes a great snack for kids; just serve it as is, or mix it in with some nuts and raisins. Throw it into granola to make it especially wonderful. Or, fold the crumble into chocolate ice cream with some bananas and nuts for your own version of Chunky Monkey!

Mise en Place

You'll find Brownie Pointers throughout the book. These are helpful hints for working with brownies or adapting a particular recipe for a variety of uses.

The single most useful Brownie Pointer is *mise en place*.

Mise en place is French for "to put in place," or Get Organized! It is a practice used by all professional cooks. In fact, if you watch chefs on television, all those little dishes are nothing more than a *mise en place*. Without it, you risk forgetting an ingredient, and/or making assembly more complicated and time-consuming than necessary. Of course, those TV chefs have dedicated minions who do all their work for them, but you can pretend that you're a TV chef—or working for one—as you do the prep and the final assembly! It's a way of organizing yourself so that baking (and cooking) can become a series of simple steps, accomplished by taking your prepared ingredients and putting them together as detailed in the recipe. It also assures consistency of results, time after time.

Here's how you set up your *mise en place*:

- Read the recipe from start to finish. I can't tell you how many times I've started a recipe only to find I lacked an ingredient, or the time, to finish it properly. Or worst of all, there are times I've realized to my horror that I've already added an ingredient without proper whipping, melting, halving, etc.!
- Measure or weigh out all your ingredients and place them in bowls on your work surface so you can be sure you haven't forgotten anything. You'd be amazed how failing to do this may lead you to omit ingredients like vanilla, salt, sometimes even eggs!

- Process the ingredients as required: bring your eggs to room temperature, zest your lemons, toast your nuts, melt your butter, etc., so you aren't scrambling at the last minute to get that lemon zested while your batter sits, deflating.

Once you become accustomed to using this technique, you'll find that every recipe becomes much faster to produce—and not just baking recipes.

Another aspect of *mise en place* is a stocked larder and freezer. All pastry chefs worth their salt have larders stocked with component parts which, when assembled, make knockout desserts in a matter of minutes. This means that you may have to take an hour or two one rainy day to make some basic recipes, but in sacrificing this initial time, you'll have saved yourself endless future hours of assembling a cookie dough or waiting for ganache to cool or pastry to chill.

You're now ready to go. Chapter One provides you with great recipes to fill your larder so you can quickly assemble the recipes in the later chapters. Not one of these recipes takes more than 15 minutes to make. With all or some of these items available, you'll be able to assemble desserts at a moment's notice that will leave your family and friends not only begging for more but wondering how you were able to do it without breaking out into hives of anxiety! Plus, your inner artist will suddenly appear—having all these ready-to-use components will make you want to experiment with new combinations and permutations.

Or, if you prefer, just jump in and go straight to Chapter Two where the brownies are. Don't forget to lick the bowl and have fun!

21 Tasty Things to Do with Brownies

Many of the following make use of ganache; see the recipe on page 13.

1. **PETITS FOURS:** Cut baked brownies into small cubes, dip into ganache and drizzle with melted white chocolate.

2. **TWO-BITE BROWNIES:** Pour brownie batter into mini muffin tins three-quarters full and bake, reducing the baking time by about half. Make them even better by frosting with whipped ganache.

3. **BROWNIE MERINGUE PIE:** Pour brownie batter into a greased pie plate and bake for about 20 minutes. Then top with meringue and bake an additional 10 minutes.

4. **FRESH BERRY BROWNIE TART:** Fill a tart pan with a removable bottom halfway up with brownie batter. Place on a baking sheet and bake in 300°F (150°C) oven until set, about 20–25 minutes, but still jiggly in the center. Cool. Spread with sweetened whipped cream and top with assorted fresh berries.

5. **SUMMER TRIFLE:** Cut baked brownies into cubes, and in a clear trifle bowl, layer with framboise-flavored, sweetened whipped cream, Brownie Curd (page 8), fresh raspberries and sliced toasted almonds.

6. **WINTER PARFAIT:** Layer crumbled brownies with rum-flavored, sweetened whipped cream, rum-soaked raisins (along with their rum) (page 24) and toasted walnuts in champagne glasses.

7. **BROWNIE ICE CREAM:** Crumble brownies into your favorite ice cream, although vanilla, coffee, chocolate and strawberry ice creams are the best.

8. **QUICK AND EASY BROWNIE FRUITCAKE:** Mix 1 cup (250 mL) Rummed Dried Fruit (page 24) into 3 cups (750 mL) of your favorite brownie batter. Pour into mini loaf pans and bake at 300°F (150°C) until slightly firm, about 30 minutes. Brush with rum when they come out of the oven. Also yummy made into mini-muffins.

9. **VALENTINE BROWNIES:** Make and chill a brownie slab. Turn upside down on a cutting board. Cut out brownie hearts with a cookie cutter. You don't have to waste the scraps; crumble them and squoosh into the cookie cutter—it will hold its heart shape. Chill. Dip the brownie hearts into ganache and chill on a rack. Using colored frosting in a piping bag, write love notes on the tops of the brownies, and place them in ruffled white muffin cups.

10. **MINT JULEP BROWNIES:** Make mint ganache (page 14) and pour over a brownie slab. Chill, cut and serve with rum raisin ice cream.

11. **CHRISTMAS BROWNIES:** Crush 2 cups (500 mL) peppermint candies or candy canes into bite-sized pieces, setting aside about ¼ cup (60 mL). Mix the candies into your favorite brownie batter, and sprinkle the remaining candies on top before baking.

12. **EASTER BROWNIES:** Bake your favorite batter in a mini Easter egg pan. Remove the brownie eggs from the pan and chill them in the refrigerator. Dip in ganache. Decorate with colored royal icing.

13. **JULY 4TH BROWNIES:** Make and chill a slab of your favorite brownies. Top with ganache. While the ganache is still a bit tacky, make an American flag on top by using rows of red raspberries and piped whipped cream for the stripes (or rows of red and yellow raspberries, if you can find them), and more whipped cream and blueberries for the stars.

14. **HALLOWEEN BROWNIES:** Make Worms 'n Dirt Parfaits by layering crumbled brownies (dirt) with gummy worms wiggling around in sweetened whipped cream dusted with cocoa.

15. **CHRISTMAS BROWNIE TRIFLE:** In a clear, flat-bottomed bowl layer brownie cubes, whipped cream

flavored with kirsch and almond extract, sour cherries in syrup, toasted slivered almonds and chopped chocolate.

16. **BROWNIE ANNIVERSARY CAKE:** Bake your favorite brownie batter in two 4-inch (10 cm) round cake pans. Cool on a wire rack, then chill in the refrigerator. Place 1 brownie layer upside down on a wire rack set on a baking tray lined with parchment paper. Pour warm ganache evenly over the top and sides. Chill and carefully transfer to a serving plate. Cut a 3-inch (7.5 cm) round from the other cake layer (keeping the crumbs). Pour ganache evenly over its top and sides. Chill. Center the second layer on top of the first. Crumble and roll the reserved brownie crumbs into 2 truffle-sized balls. Dip in ganache and chill. Place side by side on top of the top layer. Ring the bottom of the cake with fresh raspberries, and lightly dust the entire cake with icing sugar and then cocoa.

17. **BROWNIE BACCI BALLS:** Take chunks off a slab of baked brownies and form them into large truffle-sized balls. Chill. Soften your choice of ice cream or sorbet. Place a scoop in a bowl that's a bit larger than the brownie ball. Push the ball into the ice cream, and then cover completely with more ice cream. Put the brownie ice cream balls into a baking pan in the freezer. Chill for at least an hour. Warm a large amount of ganache just enough for it to be liquid. Immerse 1 bacci ball at a time in the ganache and immediately put back in the freezer. When ready to serve, dust lightly with cocoa.

18. **BROWNIE ICE CREAM PÂTÉ:** Line an 8- × 4-inch (20 × 10 cm) loaf pan with plastic wrap. Cut 3 slabs of brownies to fit lengthwise in the pan. Soften your favorite ice cream and mix with lots of chopped toasted nuts and bittersweet chocolate chunks. Line the bottom of the pan with the first brownie slab and spread enough ice cream to form a layer the same thickness as the brownie slab. Top with another layer of brownie and then ice cream, finishing with the final brownie slab. (You may have to freeze the pan between layers.) Freeze overnight. The next day, remove from the freezer and turn upside down on a cooling rack set on a baking tray lined with parchment paper. Pour lots of ganache, warmed just enough to make it liquid, over the top and sides of the pâté. Return to the freezer for at least an hour. Decorate the bottom with finely chopped nuts around the perimeter.

19. **BIGGER, BETTER S'MORES:** Place a few graham crackers on a baking sheet. Top each one with a smooshed brownie. Top with a few marshmallows. Place under the broiler until the marshmallows are slightly puffy and golden brown. Drizzle with ganache and serve immediately.

20. **ADULT SMOOTHIE:** Place some fine whisky, vanilla ice cream and a brownie into a blender. Blend until smooth. Eat with a spoon!

21. **BROWNIE SHORTCAKE:** Sauté and caramelize sliced bananas in butter and brown sugar. Deglaze the pan with a little rum. Don't let the bananas get too soft. Place a warmed brownie on a plate, then top with vanilla ice cream and the caramelized bananas. Sprinkle with toasted, chopped pecans.

Warm and Oozy, Crispy, Crunchy Brownie Building Blocks

SHINY CHOCOLATE GLAZE

YIELD: SCANT 2 CUPS (500 ML)

This is a sensational chocolate glaze that stays shiny whether refrigerated or not. Freeze it, but don't refrigerate it for longer than a few weeks or it may grow green furry things that are only suitable for your kid's science project.

½ cup (125 mL) coffee or water

⅓ cup (65 g) sugar

6 oz (170 g) bittersweet chocolate, chopped

2 Tbsp (30 mL) corn syrup

2 Tbsp (30 mL) butter

2 tsp (10 mL) coffee or vanilla extract

1. Over medium heat, warm the coffee, sugar and chocolate in a medium saucepan.

2. Add the corn syrup and bring to a boil. Boil for 5 minutes, stirring once or twice.

3. Remove from the heat. Add the butter and coffee extract.

4. Pour into a bowl. Let cool to room temperature, at which point it will thicken. If you pour it over a cake before it has cooled, it will slide off! If it thickens too much, place over hot water to warm gently.

> **BROWNIE POINTER**
>
> This makes a great base for a quick and easy hot chocolate. Heat milk and stir in 2 heaping tablespoonfuls of glaze. Top with marshmallows!

PÂTE SUCRÉE

YIELD: FOUR 9-INCH (23 CM) FLAN SHELLS

This is the recipe that M. Seurre gave me when I left my "stage" apprenticeship in Paris. Every day I would arrive, eager as ever, with my little notebook and turquoise pen, ready to copy down as many recipes as I could during our "pause café" of instant coffee, because the rest of the time they worked me tirelessly and I was happy to oblige. On my last day, the crew presented me with a wonderful book with all their recipes neatly typed but, as is typical of professionals, with no instructions. I always have a disc of both this dough and its chocolate version (see page 5) in my freezer, ready to defrost at a moment's notice when I see wonderful fruit in the store. This is a large quantity; if you want a smaller amount, divide the recipe by four and use a single egg.

1 lb + 4 Tbsp (510 g) butter, cold

2 cups (240 g) icing sugar

3 eggs

7¾ cups (1 kg) pastry flour

1 tsp (5 mL) baking powder

pinch kosher salt

1. Cut the butter into tablespoon-size pieces and place in the bowl of an electric mixer fitted with the paddle attachment.

2. Add the icing sugar and toss to coat the butter.

3. On low speed, mix the butter and the sugar together until blended. Scrape the bottom of the bowl.

4. Add the eggs 1 at a time, on low speed, scraping the bowl often.

5. Add the remaining dry ingredients and mix until the dough just comes together. It may be a bit sticky.

6. Turn the dough out onto a lightly floured surface and gently knead it for about 30 seconds.

7. Divide it into 4 pieces, press into flat discs and wrap individually in plastic. Refrigerate until firm before rolling.

8. If freezing, wrap in foil. If you have extra flan pans, line the bottom and sides with rolled dough, wrap the pan first in plastic and then foil and freeze. When ready to use, defrost in the fridge and bake as directed in your recipe.

9. Remove the dough from the fridge about 15 minutes before you want to roll it. When you are ready to roll out the disc, lightly flour your work surface. If you need the dough in a hurry, take the cold disc and gently pound it from side to side with a rolling pin. This will soften it enough to roll.

10. Roll the dough to slightly larger than the diameter of the pan plus 2 times the height. For a 9- × 4-inch (23 × 10 cm) rectangular pan, for example, roll it to about 11 × 6 inches (28 × 15 cm). For a 9-inch (23 cm) round pan, roll it into a circle of about 11 inches (28 cm) in diameter.

continued on next page . . .

Pâte Sucrée (continued)

BROWNIE POINTER

When rolling dough, use a large, flat metal spatula or removable bottom of a flan pan to loosen the dough from the work surface before turning the dough or sprinkling more flour beneath it. This way you won't tear the pastry when you move it.

The dough is easiest to work with when it's cool and almost leathery in feel. If it gets too warm and sticky, place the rolled portion on a cookie sheet and refrigerate until chilled enough to roll.

11. Fold the dough in half and lay it in the middle of the pan. Unfold and gently press the dough down the sides to meet the bottom at a right angle. If there are thin areas along the sides, fold or press any excess dough down into the sides to increase the thickness. If the sides are too thick, press the dough against the side of the pan to thin it. Use a paring knife set at an angle to trim the crust flush with the top of the pan.

12. Place in the fridge to chill completely, at least 30 minutes, before baking.

13. Depending upon your recipe, use as is or bake blind. To blind bake, preheat the oven to 350°F (180°C). Prick the bottom pastry all over with a fork, line the pastry with foil and fill with dried beans or other weights. Bake for about 10–15 minutes (or as detailed in the recipe) until lightly golden brown, if further baking is required after it is filled. Bake completely to a rich, golden brown if the shell is to be filled after baking.

14. Cool before filling.

Brownie Sandwich Cookies

Roll 1 round of dough to ⅛-inch (2 mm) thickness. Use a cookie cutter with a 2-inch (5 cm) diameter to cut out rounds. Using the small end of a large, plain piping tube, cut out holes in the middle of half the rounds. Roll out the scraps for additional cookies. Place all the rounds on a parchment-lined baking pan and bake at 350°F (180°C) for about 10 minutes or until barely golden brown around the edges. Cool. Turn the circles without holes upside down. Pipe or spoon 1 tsp (5 mL) of Brownie Curd (page 8) into the middle of these rounds. Dust the tops with holes with a good coating of icing sugar. Place them on top of the Brownie Curd. Some of the filling will ooze into the hole, but that's how you want it!

PÂTE SUCRÉE AU CHOCOLAT

YIELD: SIX 4-INCH (10 CM) TARTLETS OR TWO 8-INCH (20 CM) FLAN SHELLS

This chocolate version isn't very sweet but provides a pleasant sharpness for the fillings suggested below. The dough gets sticky when it warms up. Roll it between 2 pieces of parchment paper (or Silpat liners) to make handling easier. If it gets too soft, just return the dough, between the pieces of paper, to the fridge. Let it firm up before rolling or cutting.

½ cup + 2 Tbsp (140 g) butter

¾ cup (90 g) icing sugar

1 Tbsp (15 mL) granulated sugar

1 egg yolk

1¾ cups (225 g) pastry flour

½ cup (55 g) cocoa

pinch kosher salt

1. Cut the butter into 10 pieces (if not already in tablespoons) and place in the bowl of an electric mixer fitted with the paddle attachment.

2. Add both sugars and toss to coat the butter.

3. On low speed, mix the butter and sugars together until blended. Scrape the bottom of the bowl.

4. Add the egg yolk on low speed, and scrape the bowl.

5. Whisk the flour, cocoa and salt together.

6. Add to the butter mixture and blend until the dough just comes together. It may be a bit sticky.

7. Press into a flat disc and wrap in plastic. Refrigerate for at least 30 minutes before using.

8. If freezing, wrap in plastic and then foil. Or line a flan pan with the rolled dough, wrap it in plastic and foil and freeze. It will be ready at a moment's notice when you need it.

9. When you are ready to roll out the disc, lightly flour your work surface. Remove the dough from the fridge about 15 minutes before you want to roll it.

10. Roll the dough to about 2 inches (5 cm) larger than the diameter of your tart pan.

11. Fold the dough in half and lay it in the middle of the pan. Unfold and gently press the dough down the sides to meet the bottom at a right angle. If there are thin areas along the sides, fold or press any excess dough down into the sides to increase the thickness. If the sides are too thick, press the dough against the side of the pan to thin it. Use a paring knife set at an angle to trim the dough flush with the top of the pan.

12. Place in the fridge to chill completely, at least 30 minutes, before baking.

continued on next page . . .

13. Depending on your recipe, use as is or bake blind. To blind bake, preheat the oven to 350°F (180°C). Prick the bottom of the pastry all over with a fork, line the pastry with foil and fill with dried beans or other weights. Bake for about 10–15 minutes (or as detailed in the recipe) until it looks and feels firm. Chocolate pastry is notoriously difficult to gauge but it's always better to underbake than overbake.

14. Cool before filling.

Chocolate Sandwich Cookies

Instead of patting the dough into a disc, roll it into a log 1½ inches (4 cm) in diameter. Wrap roll in plastic, then foil, label and freeze. When you need a quick cookie, slice into ⅛-inch-thick (2 mm) rounds, chill for 15 minutes, and bake at 325°F (160°C) for 8–10 minutes or until just crisp around the edges. (Alternatively, roll out the dough to a ⅛-inch (2 mm) thickness and cut out desired shape with a cookie cutter.) Cool and pipe or spread Brownie Curd (page 8) on the bottom of 1 cookie. Top with a second cookie. Dust with icing sugar.

Délice au Chocolat

Roll the dough to ⅛-inch (2 mm) thickness. Use a 3-inch (7.5 cm) scalloped cookie cutter to cut out 6 discs. Chill for 15 minutes. Bake at 350°F (180°C) for 8–10 minutes. Cool. Pipe Brownie Curd (page 8), as is or lightened with some whipped cream, or whipped ganache (page 13) into the center, leaving some room at the edges. Place fresh raspberries in a circle around the edges. Top with another cookie and press down slightly. Pipe a rosette of filling on top and press a fresh raspberry and mint leaf in at a rakish angle. Dust lightly with icing sugar.

Key Lime Chocolate Tarts (pictured)

Roll out dough and line six 4-inch (10 cm) tart shells, chill for 15 minutes, line with foil and fill with pie weights or beans. Bake until three-quarters done (about 10 minutes for small tarts; 12–15 minutes for larger tarts). While they're baking, whisk together 2 eggs, 1 egg yolk, ¾ cup + 2 Tbsp sugar (175 g), 3 Tbsp (45 mL) key lime juice, ½ tsp (2 mL) baking powder and ¼ tsp (1 mL) kosher salt. Remove the foil and pie weights and fill each tart shell almost to the brim. Bake in a 300°F (150°C) oven for about 20 minutes or until the filling is no longer liquid. Sprinkle the top with strips of lime rind or toasted coconut.

BROWNIE CURD

YIELD: SCANT 2 CUPS (500 ML)

There's lemon curd and lime curd, and there's vanilla custard and chocolate custard, but no one, to my knowledge, has ever created a brownie curd! Gorgeously dark and not too sweet, this is a wonderful spread on cinnamon toast, and a wonderful filling for prebaked tart shells. Best of all, properly stored it has a long shelf life, so you can pull it out of the fridge and create something spontaneous with very little effort.

1 cup (250 mL) whipping cream

1 vanilla bean, sliced in half lengthwise

½ cup (55 g) cocoa

½ cup (100 g) sugar

3 egg yolks

1 whole egg

¼ tsp (1 mL) kosher salt

1 Tbsp (15 mL) butter

2½ oz (70 g) bittersweet chocolate, chopped

1. Place the cream and vanilla bean in a medium saucepan. Bring to a low simmer and turn off the heat. Let sit for 30 minutes.

2. Using the tip of a knife, scrape out the seeds from the bean into the cream. Remove the bean, rinse and place in your sugar jar to flavor your sugar.

3. Add the cocoa to the vanilla cream and whisk to blend.

4. Place the saucepan over medium heat and heat just until you see bubbles around the edges.

5. In another bowl, whisk together the sugar, egg yolks, egg and salt.

6. Gradually whisk the warm cream into the eggs and sugar (wrap a tea towel around the bottom of the bowl so the bowl doesn't move while you pour and whisk at the same time).

7. Place a sieve over the saucepan and pour the curd mixture back into the pan, discarding whatever is left in the sieve.

8. Return the pan to the heat and mix constantly with a wooden spoon. The mixture must not boil! Keep mixing until you feel and see the curd thickening. You will feel resistance to your stirring. From time to time, remove the pan from the heat and stir, keeping an eye on the mixture to make sure it's not boiling or burning on the bottom.

9. When the curd has thickened to the consistency of sour cream, remove from the heat and stir in the butter and chopped chocolate. Mix to blend thoroughly. (Or, pour the curd into the bowl of a food processor and, with the motor running, add the butter and chocolate bit by bit. Process until completely smooth.) Let cool, about 5 minutes.

10. At this point, you may pour the curd directly into prebaked tart shells (see Brownie Curd Raspberry Tarts) or place in a sealed container with a piece of plastic wrap set directly on the surface of the curd to keep it moist.

11. Store in the fridge for up to 3 weeks.

Here are just a few suggestions for ways to use Brownie Curd:

- Stir ¼ cup (60 mL) curd into a cup of hot milk (or better yet, hot cream!) for the best hot chocolate ever.

- Mix ¼ cup (60 mL) curd with 3 Tbsp (45 mL) whipping cream to thin. Fold into 1 cup (250 mL) whipped cream for a quick mousse.

- Mix ¾ cup (185 mL) curd with 2 Tbsp (30 mL) whipping cream. Pour into pre-baked tart shells and let set. Garnish with berries and/or crème fraîche.

- Spread between layers of angel food cake.

- Place curd in a small piping bag fitted with a #2 or #5 plain tip. Pipe into the hollow end of raspberries for an outrageously extravagant end to an elegant meal.

- Mix with equal amounts of warmed raspberry jam for an extra-special breakfast spread.

Brownie Curd Raspberry Tarts

Fill six 4-inch (10 cm) baked Pâte Sucrée (page 3) or Pâte Sucrée au Chocolat tart shells (page 5) with warm Brownie Curd. Place fresh raspberries (about 1 pint/150 g) in concentric circles on top, starting from the outside edge and covering the entire surface. Dust lightly with icing sugar.

Peanut Butter Brownie Curd Spread

Mix equal amounts of smooth peanut butter and Brownie Curd together. Make sure they are both at room temperature. Use as a filling for sandwich cookies (see Pâte Sucrée au Chocolat, page 5, or Chocolate Rugelah, page 140).

Brownie Curd Praline Spread

Mix together equal amounts of praline paste (available from gourmet stores) and Brownie Curd. Use to fill cookies or tarts or fold it into whipped cream for a complex and utterly delicious mousse.

MASCARPONE CHOCOLATE CURD

YIELD: 4½ CUPS (1.125 L)

If you haven't already made the recipe for Brownie Curd (page 8), then shame on you! However, it's never too late to discover the wonderful versatility of chocolate curd. One of my testers said this recipe was so good that I should tell everyone to double it. So, go ahead, double it and give it away to your best friends, or store it in the fridge where it will remain delicious for a long time, as long as you place plastic wrap flush with the top and seal it tightly in a container.

1 lb (454 g) bittersweet chocolate chips

2 cups (500 mL) mascarpone cheese or sour cream

5 Tbsp (70 g) butter

4 eggs, lightly beaten

pinch kosher salt

1. Place the chocolate, mascarpone and butter in a medium saucepan over low heat. Stir gently until it is all melted.

2. Remove the pan from the heat and quickly whisk in the eggs, being sure that you whisk briskly to incorporate them before they have a chance to cook and curdle.

3. Return the pan to low heat and stir until the mixture thickens, again being careful not to cook to the boiling point.

4. Pour the curd through a fine sieve into a bowl, using a rubber spatula to press it through.

5. Stir in the salt.

6. Store in a sealed container with a piece of plastic wrap flush with the surface of the curd to keep it moist. Refrigerate.

7. Reheat by placing curd in a bowl over gently simmering water until it liquefies.

BROWNIE POINTERS

- Use as an ultrarich pudding, all on its own.

- Pour into espresso cups and chill or serve warm, topped with a swirl of sweetened whipped cream.

- Spread between cake layers or cookies.

- Fill meringue cups and surround with berries.

- Make peanut butter and mascarpone curd French toast: Mix equal amounts of curd and peanut butter; sandwich between 2 pieces of egg bread; dip in beaten egg and fry until golden in lots of butter. Serve with fresh raspberries or a raspberry purée.

Any way you serve it, it is wonderful.

Rich Chocolate Crumble
YIELD: ABOUT 3½ CUPS (875 ML)

I don't know any baked good that can't be improved by adding crumble: even my brownies hit the stratosphere of taste when a thick layer of these crunchy, sandy crumbs go on top. Try them on tarts, on fruit crumbles, on muffins, on ice cream, on just about anything!

½ cup (115 g) butter at room temperature

½ cup (100 g) sugar

1 cup *less* 2 Tbsp (115 g) all-purpose flour

3 Tbsp (25 g) whole wheat flour

¼ cup (30 g) cocoa

1 tsp (5 mL) cinnamon

½ tsp (2 mL) kosher salt

¼ tsp (1 mL) freshly grated nutmeg

2⅛ oz (60 g) whole almonds, toasted

2½ oz (70 g) bittersweet chocolate

1. Place all ingredients in the bowl of a food processor fitted with the steel blade.

2. Pulse on and off until the nuts are finely chopped.

3. Squeeze handfuls on top of your chosen dessert.

4. Store any unused crumble in a tightly sealed container in the freezer for up to 1 year.

BROWNIE POINTERS

- All nuts are good in this crumble—hazelnuts, pecans and walnuts in particular. Make sure they are toasted first for maximum flavor. On the other hand, if you don't like nuts or want a nut-free crumble you can substitute an equal amount of toasted oatmeal or just leave them out altogether.

- If you prefer your crumble crunchier, place the nuts in the processor bowl after you pulse the rest of the ingredients. Pulse only until the nuts are in small pieces, and not finely chopped.

- If you prefer even crunchier crumbs, melt the butter, but let it cool. Add the butter and then the chocolate only after pulsing the rest of the ingredients.

- Turn this into a cake all by itself: Press half the crumbs into a parchment-lined 9-inch (23 cm) round cake pan. Crumble the remaining crumbs into marble-sized pieces and gently press into the bottom layer. Bake for about 20 minutes at 350°F (150°C) or until fragrant. Cool. Drizzle with ganache (page 13) and dust with icing sugar before serving.

GANACHE

YIELD: 4 CUPS (1 L)

Ganache is French for a combination of cream and chocolate. It's one of the simplest things to make and one of the most versatile. It's also the filling and glaze for truffles. Make sure that you use cream as fresh as you can get it, preferably organic, and the best chocolate you can afford. Don't be afraid to experiment by infusing the hot cream with flavors like vanilla bean, fresh mint, grated ginger or cinnamon. Heat the cream, add the flavoring and let sit for an hour or so, then strain. You'll have to reheat the cream before completing the ganache. My ganache varies depending upon whether or not I want it thinner (add more cream or reduce the chocolate) or shiny (add some corn syrup), but it always starts with equal amounts of chocolate and cream by weight. I portion out the recipe into four containers, label and freeze them so I always have some glaze, or chocolate "sauce," available to jazz up a dessert.

2 cups (500 mL) whipping cream

1 lb (454 g) bittersweet chocolate, chopped

1. Heat the cream to just below a boil, when bubbles appear around the edges of the saucepan.

2. Pour it over the chopped chocolate and let sit for 5 minutes.

3. Gently whisk until smooth. Try not to create air bubbles.

4. To use as a glaze, cool (or reheat) to between 80–85°F (27–30°C).

◄ The Classic Brownie (page 29) with Ganache (this page)

continued on next page . . .

Ganache (continued)

Ganache is incredibly versatile:

• To use it as mousse, make recipe without adding any corn syrup or coffee. Place in the fridge until cold but not solid, and beat with the whisk attachment of an electric mixer until light and fluffy. Don't overmix or it will become grainy. You want it smooth. Use as you would a mousse: as a cake filling, as a base for a parfait, as a filling between cookies.

• For truffle filling, use a 2-to-1 ratio of chocolate to cream, and add a quarter of the weight of the chocolate in butter. Pour into a parchment-lined jelly roll pan and refrigerate until completely firm. Using a teaspoon or a scoop, form into balls and place on another parchment-lined sheet. Refrigerate until firm. Roll quickly into balls and return to the fridge. Roll in cocoa, chopped nuts or icing sugar or dip into melted but cooled chocolate.

• To use as chocolate sauce, reheat ganache gently in a shallow hot water bath. Flavor with liqueur and serve over ice cream and brownies to make a "brownie sundae."

• For glaze, let your brownies (or cake) cool in the pan, then chill completely. Pour the ganache on top and tilt the pan so the ganache covers the top completely and evenly. Let cool. Dip a tea towel in hot water and squeeze it dry. Wrap it around the edges of the pan. When the ganache starts melting around the edges, lift out the brownie slab or open the springform surrounding the cake. You will have clean edges. Slice with a hot knife wiped clean after every cut.

• For a professional gloss and expert finishing touch, drizzle ganache over cookies, cakes and pies (such as pecan).

• Put warm ganache into a squeeze bottle and make wonderful designs by spreading Crème Anglaise (facing page) on serving plate and drizzling concentric circles of ganache overtop. Use a toothpick or knife tip to "pull" the chocolate from the center towards the edges of the plate at 1-inch (2.5 cm) intervals. Place your dessert in the center of this "web."

• Vary the flavors of your ganache by reducing the cream by a tablespoon or two (15 or 30 mL) and substituting liqueurs such as Grand Marnier (orange), Kahlúa (coffee) or even straight whisky or rum. Don't be afraid to experiment!

• Infuse your cream first with different herbs and spices: simmer the cream with ¼ cup (60 mL) minced fresh mint leaves (or up to 1 tsp peppermint extract, depending upon how minty you want it), 1 Tbsp (15 mL) chai tea spices or 2 cinnamon sticks or 2 tsp (10 mL) Earl Grey tea and let sit for about 15 minutes. Return to just below the boil and strain over the chocolate. Whisk until smooth.

CRÈME ANGLAISE

YIELD: SCANT 3 CUPS (750 ML)

This is another recipe M. Seurre and his team gave me when I completed my apprenticeship at Patisserie Seurre. He was so generous with all his recipes that I feel it a duty to pass them on for others to enjoy. Use this as a sauce or garnish for everything from brownies to cakes to tarts and berries.

2 cups (500 mL) milk

1 vanilla bean, split lengthwise

4 egg yolks

⅔ cup (130 g) sugar

BROWNIE POINTER

For flavored Crème Anglaise, omit the vanilla and replace with a tablespoonful of your favorite liqueur.

1. In a medium saucepan on medium heat, bring the milk and vanilla bean to just under a boil. You will see little bubbles around the edges. Steam will begin to rise from the surface.

2. Meanwhile, whisk together the egg yolks and sugar.

3. Pour one-quarter of the hot milk into the egg yolk/sugar mixture, whisking rapidly so the eggs don't cook, but are heated through.

4. Pour the egg/milk mixture into the saucepan with the remaining milk and whisk to blend.

5. Return the pot to low heat and stir constantly with a wooden spoon until it begins to thicken. Do not let it boil or the eggs will cook and the mixture will curdle.

6. The cream is ready when you can run your finger across the back of the spoon and the cream remains in place on either side of the track.

7. Strain the cream into a clean bowl. Remove the vanilla bean. Use the tip of a knife to scrape all the seeds into the Crème Anglaise. (Rinse the vanilla bean and put it into your sugar bin for vanilla-infused sugar.)

8. Cover with plastic wrap pressed onto the surface of the crème to keep it moist. Seal tightly. Chill if not using immediately.

CRÈME D'AMANDE

YIELD: 3 CUPS (750 ML)

This classic French filling is a recipe you'll use again and again, and not just with brownies. It can be doubled or tripled and frozen for up to a year. This makes a large quantity but you can easily halve it.

½ lb (227 g) butter at room temperature

½ lb (227 g) sugar

½ lb (227 g) ground almonds

3 eggs at room temperature, lightly beaten

1 tsp (5 mL) almond extract

1. Place the butter in the bowl of an electric mixer fitted with the paddle attachment. Beat until softened, about 3 minutes.

2. With the machine on low speed add the sugar. Increase the speed to medium and beat until light and fluffy, about 4 minutes. Scrape down the sides and bottom as required.

3. Add the ground almonds and beat just until incorporated.

4. With the machine on low speed, add the eggs in a slow but steady stream. Scrape the sides and bottom of the bowl.

5. Add the almond extract. Increase the speed to medium and beat until light and fluffy.

6. Use immediately, or store in a covered container in the freezer.

> **BROWNIE POINTER**
>
> This recipe is extremely good if you use toasted almonds with the skin still on. Other nuts may also be substituted—especially good are hazelnuts and walnuts.

Chocolate Frangipane Fresh Berry Tart

Line a 7.5-inch (19 cm) tart pan with Pâte Sucrée au Chocolat (page 5). (You will need about half the recipe.) Prick with a fork. Line with foil and weight with beans or weights to keep the pastry from shrinking. Bake at 350°F (180°C) for 12 minutes. Remove the foil and weights. Spread ¾ cup (185 mL) of the crème filling to ¼ inch (5 mm) below the top. Press ½ pint (75 g) fresh raspberries into the crème. Return to the oven and bake until the filling is slightly puffed and set, about 20–25 minutes. Cool. Warm ½ cup (125 mL) ganache (page 13). Pour over the top of the cooled tart and tip and turn the tart gently so the chocolate covers the entire surface. Serve as is or generously cover the surface either neatly or randomly with fresh raspberries. Dust with icing sugar and serve.

Hazelnut Cherry Chocolate Tart

Make the crème, substituting toasted, skinned hazelnuts for the almonds. Line a 7.5-inch (19 cm) tart pan with Pâte Sucrée (page 3). Prick with a fork. Line with foil and beans or weights to keep the pastry from shrinking. Bake at 350°F (180°C) for 12 minutes. Remove the foil and weights. Spread ¾ cup (185 mL) of the crème filling to ¼ inch (5 mm) below the top. Dot the filling with fresh, pitted sour cherries. Sprinkle with cinnamon sugar and return to the oven until the crème is barely firm and slightly golden brown, about 20–25 minutes. Drizzle the top with ganache (page 13) and let it set. Dust with icing sugar.

Brownies à la Crème

Swirl ½ cup (125 mL) of the crème into your favorite brownie recipe. Top with ½ cup (60 g) almonds, sliced and tossed gently in a lightly beaten egg white and a tablespoon (15 mL) of granulated sugar. Bake at 300°F (150°C) for approximately 30–40 minutes or until it's slightly puffed in the center and the top is golden with shiny almonds. Voilà! A dense, moist center with a crispy, crackly topping.

Caramel Butterscotch Sauce

YIELD: SCANT 2 CUPS (500 ML)

When I was a kid, I could never decide which sauce was better: a gooey caramel, or hot fudge. So I usually had both. This and the Chocolate Fudge Sauce (see facing page) are among my favorite recipes because they can be used over ice cream, in brownies or drizzled on a plate to dazzle your friends and family. Personalize this recipe by deciding to what degree you like your sugar caramelized: really dark, so it gets a bitter edge that some people crave; or golden, so the flavor is more mellow. Just be sure that you don't completely burn the sugar . . . it will smoke when it begins to burn and you'll have to open all your windows, throw out the mess and start again. This recipe is unusual as it uses crème fraîche. You can easily replace it with an equal amount of whipping cream.

1 cup (200 g) sugar

2 Tbsp (30 mL) corn syrup

½ cup (125 mL) whipping cream

¼ cup (60 mL) crème fraîche

¼–½ tsp (1–2 mL) kosher salt

2 Tbsp (30 mL) butter (optional)

1 Tbsp (15 mL) Scotch (optional, but good!)

BROWNIE POINTERS

• Warm the sauce before using over ice cream and don't forget a sprinkling of salt on top. Simply out of this world.

• Don't have much time? Dump all the ingredients into a heavy saucepan and bring to a boil over medium heat, stirring constantly. Boil for about 5 minutes. You won't get the same intensity of flavor but the sauce will be very, very good all the same.

1. Place the sugar and corn syrup in a heavy, deep 1 quart (1 liter) saucepan over medium heat.

2. Stir with a wooden spoon until the sugar is dissolved. It will be sticky and lumpy at first. Break up the lumps with a wooden spoon and bring the mixture to a rolling boil. Place the lid on the pan for about 1 minute to allow the steam to dissolve any sugar crystals on the sides of the pan. Remove the lid.

3. For the first 10 minutes or so, you will have a lively, bubbling liquid. The bubbles will break with ease but gradually the mixture will thicken, the bubbles will start to slow down and you will hardly hear them bursting. Like an unruly child whose energy is spent, you will see the sugar subside to a quiet simmer. Eventually, the sugar will begin to darken in color.

4. Pay attention! The sugar caramelizes quickly now. Swirl the pan to distribute the caramelized sugar evenly. If it begins to darken too quickly, remove the pan from the heat.

5. When it reaches a rich, deep, golden brown, remove the pan from the heat and carefully add the whipping cream and crème fraîche, standing away from the pan to avoid being splattered and burned. The mixture will boil up furiously and produce prodigious amounts of steam. Keep your hands and face away from the volcanic action!

6. Return the pan to low heat and stir to dissolve any coagulated sugar. When completely smooth, remove from the heat and add the salt. (The French make a wonderful salted caramel. Notice how wonderful this tastes if you use ½ tsp [2 ml] of salt!) Add the butter and Scotch, if using.

7. Let cool a bit before storing in a sealed container. This sauce has an indefinite shelf life and may be frozen. If it separates, just stir it back together. If it hardens, soften in a saucepan over low heat.

CHOCOLATE FUDGE SAUCE

YIELD: 2 CUPS (500 ML)

*My mother, Elaine, a fabulous impromptu cook, always used to make Baked Alaska for
New Year's Eve, and everything was last minute, including the hot fudge sauce. She never used
a recipe and as a result there were some years when the sauce was thick and flowing and other
years when it congealed like lava over Pompeii, threatening a midnight rush to the dentist for
a removed filling. Happily, that never happened, since we all learned to suck the pieces of hot fudge
that we pried off the ice cream and the plate as if they were Tootsie Rolls. You shouldn't have that
problem with this recipe unless you don't pay attention and boil it for too long.*

4 oz (113 g) unsweetened chocolate

¼ cup (60 mL) corn syrup

1 cup (250 mL) whipping cream

½ cup (100 g) granulated sugar

½ cup (110 g) brown sugar

pinch kosher salt

1. Place all the ingredients in a medium-sized heavy saucepan.

2. Bring to a boil over medium heat, stirring constantly until smooth.

3. Boil for 1 minute without stirring.

4. Remove from the heat and pour into a heatproof bowl to cool.

5. This stores indefinitely in the refrigerator or freezer in a tightly sealed container or squeeze bottle.

6. Reheat by putting it in a bowl over simmering water, or by putting the squeeze bottle (if you have stored it this way) directly into simmering water. Shake before using to make sure the entire contents have melted.

Mocha-ed Nuts (continued)

12. After 10 minutes, the top will be crisp while the bottom will still be quite moist. Using a stiff spatula, lift the nuts and turn them over. Shake to create an even layer.

13. Return to the oven. After another 10 minutes, flip the nuts again and return to the oven.

14. Bake for another 10 minutes, for a total baking time of 30 minutes.

15. Remove the nuts from the pan and let cool completely.

16. Store in an airtight tin at room temperature for up to 2 months ... but they never last that long.

RUMMED RAISINS (OR RUMMED DRIED FRUIT)

YIELD: 2 CUPS (500 ML)

These are extraordinarily good and simple. Add them to your favorite brownie recipe, the Not So Wacky Brownie Cake with Balsamic Vinegar and Marinated Strawberries (page 100) or the Ultimate, Ultimate Chocolate Chunk Cookies (page 124). Stored in a sealed jar in the fridge, they just get better and better.

2 cups (240 g) dark or yellow raisins, or assorted dried fruit such as apricots, dates, prunes, cranberries, cherries, candied peel, etc. diced into the size of raisins

1 cup (250 mL) good-quality rum

1. Place the rum and raisins (or dried fruit) in a small saucepan and bring to a boil.

2. Shake the pan to coat the raisins completely.

3. Remove from the heat and let the raisins (or dried fruit) infuse with the rum.

4. Keep away from the kids!

CHAPTER 2
Fabulously Fudgy Brownies

* These numbers denote the Fudge Factor, which indicates how comparatively moist and fudgy each brownie will be. See "Fudge Factor" on page x.

First and Foremost Brownies

YIELD: 16 BARS

I love this recipe because it's fast and fudgy and provides a stable surrounding for so many of my favorite flavors: nuts, rummed dried fruit, ginger and spices, to name just a few. The batter may be refrigerated or frozen almost indefinitely, so make twice the recipe. That way you'll always have some on hand for those pesky relatives or neighbors who keep turning up unexpectedly just to eat your famous brownies.

½ cup (115 g) butter

8 oz (227 g) bittersweet chocolate

½ cup (110 g) brown sugar

½ cup (100 g) granulated sugar

3 eggs at room temperature

2 tsp (10 mL) vanilla extract

½ cup (65 g) all-purpose flour

¼ tsp (1 mL) kosher salt

1. Preheat the oven to 300°F (150°C). Line an 8-inch (20 cm) square pan with overhanging parchment paper.

2. Melt the butter and cook until it becomes light brown and smells wonderful. Remove from the heat. Cool for 10 minutes.

3. Add the chocolate and melt. Stir until smooth.

4. Add the sugars and mix well. The mixture will be grainy.

5. Add the eggs 1 at a time, mixing until the batter is glossy and thick.

6. Add the vanilla, then the flour, mixing only enough to incorporate the flour.

7. Add the salt and mix briefly. (Adding the salt at the end of the mixing lends a wonderful contrast to the sweetness.)

8. Pour into the prepared pan and bake for 25–30 minutes. The edges will be firm but the center will be slightly soft, yet puffed. Remove from the oven and chill completely.

9. Slice into bars, wrap well and store in the fridge for up to 1 month, or in the freezer for up to 6 months.

continued on next page . . .

11. Place a cutting board over the pan and turn upside down. Remove the parchment paper.

12. If you are glazing the brownies, do so bottom side up for an entirely smooth surface.

13. If you are eating them as is, invert them onto another board and slice into cubes, rectangles or triangles.

14. Store in the fridge wrapped in plastic for up to 2–3 weeks. Freeze wrapped in plastic and foil for up to 6 months.

BROWNIE POINTERS

- The recipe makes almost 6 cups (1.5 L) of batter. Because many of my recipes call for this batter as an ingredient, you can make a smaller batch of brownies and freeze the rest of the batter. Pour the brownies into a parchment-lined 8-inch (20 cm) square baking pan, three-quarters of the way up the sides, and bake as instructed. Place the remaining batter in a freezer bag and refrigerate for up to 3 months or freeze indefinitely. Defrost before using.

- Instant flour is found in the baking section of grocery stores as "Wondra."

Gluten-Free Classic Brownies

It seems that everyone is on some form of diet these days, depriving themselves of anything from fat to wheat, carbs or cholesterol. I have experimented with a lot of ingredients to replace some of what makes brownies nutritionally "naughty" and have had good success in many cases. This variation of The Classic Brownie is a case in point. Substituting brown rice flour for wheat flour makes these entirely gluten-free, but they continue to provide a wallop of fudgy goodness. And, if it's only a few people who are wheat sensitive, you can easily adjust the recipe so that you prepare some Classic Brownies and some Gluten-free Classic Brownies with a minimum of additional effort.

Prepare the batter up to the addition of flour. Replace the wheat flour with 1 cup (130 g) of brown rice flour. Fill an 8-inch (20 cm) square pan three-quarters full with batter and bake as directed. Cool and chill completely before slicing. These are stickier than regular brownies and not quite as thick, but they're just as good!

Brownie Torte

Turn a brownie into something elegant and easy ...

1. Bake the brownies in a 9- × 13-inch (23 × 33 cm) baking pan.

2. When cool, slice lengthwise so you have 2 strips 4½ inches (12 cm) wide by 13 inches (33 cm) long.

continued on next page ...

Seville Orange Hazelnut Brownies

YIELD: 24 BARS

Seville oranges briefly come to market just when you'd welcome citrus fruits: in the depths of winter. Also known as "bitter oranges," they are unlike their more beverage friendly cousins. Rather than a juice that entices through lush sweetness, these seductive orbs beckon with a sharp bite and a lingering bitterness that cleave to the sides of your tongue. You either love them or hate them. I love them, especially in thick, sticky marmalade for which they are uniquely suited since their skins are heavily laced with pectin. These brownies combine an intense homemade marmalade with a crunchy hazelnut topping to create a truly grown-up confection. Of course, if it's summer or you don't have time to make the marmalade, you can substitute a similar amount of very high quality store-bought marmalade. It won't be nearly as tasty, but it will impress nonetheless. These brownies blend sweet and sour, soft and crunchy, into a loving embrace.

Seville Orange Marmalade:

YIELD: 1½ CUPS (310 ML)

2 Seville oranges, about 3 oz/85 g each

¾ cup + 2 Tbsp (175 g) sugar

1 tsp (5 mL) vanilla extract

pinch kosher salt

1. Cut the oranges in half and remove all the seeds. Remove the little, hard brown stem too. Cut the halves into quarters.

2. Place the orange pieces, along with the sugar, in a food processor fitted with the steel blade. Pulse on and off until you have an evenly coarse mixture.

3. Scrape into a small saucepan and let sit at room temperature for about 30 minutes. A nice syrup will form.

4. Bring to a boil over medium heat, and then reduce to a simmer. Stir from time to time to make sure it doesn't burn or caramelize. If it seems to be getting dry without the rind becoming soft, add a tablespoon or two of water and continue to simmer. Be careful not to let it burn or let the sugar caramelize or else the orange intensity will be lost.

5. Cook for about 15–20 minutes or until it has thickened and the rind is soft. It will thicken further as it cools. Remove from the heat.

6. When the marmalade has cooled to room temperature, stir in the vanilla and salt.

7. Set aside ½ cup (125 mL) for the brownies, and place the rest in a glass jar. Store in the fridge and marvel at how accomplished you are. Use on toast, between cake layers, smooshed into vanilla ice cream, etc.

continued on page 40 . . .

FIVE NUTS IN A PAN BROWNIES

YIELD: 16 BARS

This recipe is an ode to everyone who loves chocolate and nuts, and to those who are simply nuts over chocolate! These are amazing brownies with a shiny surface glistening with caramel sauce bubbling over with nuts. Serve warm with vanilla or ginger ice cream and you'll be in seventh heaven.

2 oz (56 g) coarsely chopped pecans

2 oz (56 g) almonds, in any form

2 oz (56 g) whole, skinned hazelnuts

2 oz (56 g) walnut pieces

2 oz (56 g) pine nuts

4 cups (1 L) Classic Brownie batter (see page 29)

1 cup (250 mL) Caramel Butterscotch Sauce (see page 18)

BROWNIE POINTER

There are a number of techniques to remove the skin from hazelnuts, most of them really annoying. Recently, however, I discovered a quick and easy way. Place the hazelnuts on a microwaveable plate and microwave on high for about 1½ minutes. Remove and place the nuts in a clean dishtowel. Rub the nuts between your hands and the skin flakes off. For those nuts that insist on keeping their skin, just put them back in the microwave for another minute or so.

1. Preheat the oven to 300°F (150°C). Line a 9-inch (23 cm) square pan with overhanging parchment paper.

2. Place all the nuts on a baking tray and bake in the oven for 10 minutes, stirring occasionally. Remove from the oven and cool. Place in a medium-sized bowl.

3. Spread the brownie batter evenly in the prepared pan. Place in the oven and bake for 25 minutes.

4. Five minutes before the brownies are ready, heat the Caramel Butterscotch Sauce in the microwave until it is warm and liquid, about 1½ minutes. Pour the sauce over the nuts and mix gently to coat.

5. Remove the brownies from the oven and drop the nut mixture over the brownies using a soup spoon. Spread them gently in an even layer, using an offset spatula. Don't press too hard or the nuts will go into the brownies. If they go in a bit, don't worry about it. You just don't want them to be submerged.

6. Return the pan to the oven for an additional 5–7 minutes, or until the sauce starts to bubble around the edges. Don't allow it to bake too much, since it can quickly go from golden to burned.

7. Remove the brownies from the oven and cool to room temperature. Loosen the brownie slab by running a spatula around the edges before trying to remove it from the pan. Cool completely.

8. Using the overhanging parchment paper, lift the brownie slab out of the pan and admire your handiwork!

9. These brownies are best cut with a heavy chef's knife that is slightly wet. Wipe the blade clear after each slice to achieve a neat edge and a professional look.

◀ CLOCKWISE FROM TOP
The Classic Brownie with added nuts (page 29), Five Nuts in a Pan Brownies (this page), Chocolate Raspberry Peanut Butter Crumble Bars (page 58), No Bake Brownies (page 64)

EXTREME BROWNIES

YIELD: TWO 12- × 15-INCH (30 × 38 CM) PANS OR THREE 9- × 13-INCH (23 × 33 CM) PANS

You've heard of Extreme Sports—those on-the-edge, daring activities that most of us watch on TV while happily downing brownies and milk. Here's a brownie version, loaded with Rummed Raisins and cocoa nibs (tiny pieces of unprocessed cocoa beans that add crunch and a slight bitterness to every bite), not to mention pecans and chocolate. If you want them thin, bake them in the two larger pans, but if, like me, you like something substantial, divide the batter among three smaller pans for thicker bars.

1 lb (454 g) butter, divided

6½ oz (185 g) 70% bittersweet chocolate

1 lb (454 g) bittersweet chocolate

6 eggs

1 cup (200 g) granulated sugar

½ cup (110 g) dark brown or Muscovado sugar

2 Tbsp (30 mL) vanilla extract

1½ cups (200 g) whole wheat flour

1 Tbsp (15 mL) baking powder

1 tsp (5 mL) kosher salt

1½ cups (375 mL) Rummed Raisins (or Rummed Dried Fruit) (see page 24)

8 oz (227 g) pecans, toasted and cooled

1 cup (115 g) cocoa nibs

1. Preheat the oven to 300°F (150°C). Line the pans with overhanging parchment paper.

2. Place half the butter in a large saucepan and melt slowly over low heat.

3. Add the 2 chocolates when the butter is half melted. Stir occasionally to make sure the chocolate doesn't stick to the bottom and burn.

4. When the chocolate is almost completely melted, turn off the heat. Add the remaining butter, which will melt and cool the chocolates.

5. Meanwhile, stir the eggs gently with the granulated and brown sugars until blended. Add the vanilla and blend.

6. Pour the melted, cooled chocolate into a large bowl. Gradually add the sugar and eggs, stirring quickly to blend thoroughly. The mixture will be thick and glossy with an ethereal aroma. Don't get waylaid by wanting to drink it! Keep going!

7. Mix the flour with the baking powder and salt.

8. Gradually add the dry ingredients to the chocolate mixture, mixing gently but thoroughly to make a completely smooth batter.

9. Add the Rummed Raisins and any accumulated juices, along with the nuts and cocoa nibs. Mix to blend.

10. Divide the batter among the prepared pans and bake for 30 minutes, not a minute more! The top should not puff up or dome. The edges will be firm but the center will still be soft without being liquid.

11. Cool completely. Cut with a sharp, wet knife, wiping the knife between cuts. The bars may be frozen, well-wrapped in plastic and foil, for up to 6 months (and probably a lot longer!), or stored in the fridge, wrapped the same way, for weeks and weeks.

Grown-Up Rocky Road Brownies

YIELD: 16 BARS

"Rocky Road" is usually an excuse for adding just about everything to a dish, which usually ends up being extremely sweet (look who's talking!). The rum-soaked raisins, however, mean this recipe is definitely for adults and not nearly as sweet as its various namesakes.

7 Tbsp (100 g) butter

4 oz (113 g) unsweetened chocolate

4 oz (113 g) milk chocolate

¾ cup (165 g) brown sugar

1 Tbsp (15 mL) molasses

3 eggs

¼ cup (35 g) all-purpose flour

½ tsp (2 mL) kosher salt

¾ cup (175 mL) Rummed Raisins (or Rummed Dried Fruit) (see page 24)

1 cup (80 g) mini-marshmallows, divided

3 oz (85 g) walnuts, toasted and coarsely chopped

1. Preheat the oven to 300°F (150°C). Line a 9-inch (23 cm) square pan with overhanging parchment paper.

2. In a heavy saucepan melt the butter and both chocolates over low heat. Whisk until smooth.

3. Blend in the sugar and molasses.

4. Add the eggs and whisk until smooth.

5. Add the flour and salt and whisk until blended.

6. Add the raisins and half the marshmallows. Fold them in gently.

7. Pour into the prepared pan and spread until even.

8. Spread the remaining marshmallows over the top and place the walnuts in between the marshmallows to completely cover the top.

9. Bake for 35 minutes. Let cool before lifting out of the pan.

Hunky Chunkies

YIELD: 16 BARS

A big argument ensued when I brought these to the table: Did the Nestlé Chunky candy bar consist of raisins with Brazil nuts or peanuts? Older people in the family insisted it was Brazil nuts, while I, the know-it-all foodie, stuck with peanuts. It seems we were both right: Chunkys started out with Brazil nuts but when Brazil nuts became too expensive, they were replaced by peanuts. This is the brownie version of the candy bar.

Brownie Layer:

½ cup (115 g) butter

1 cup (200 g) granulated sugar

¾ cup (165 g) brown sugar

8 oz (227 g) bittersweet chocolate

¾ cup (185 mL) peanut butter

2 eggs

¼ cup (35 g) all-purpose flour

½ tsp (2 mL) kosher salt

1 recipe Peanut Butter and Raisin Layer

1. Line a 9-inch (23 cm) square pan with overhanging parchment paper.

2. In a medium saucepan, melt the butter, sugars and chocolate over medium heat. Whisk until smooth, shiny and thick. Do not let it boil.

3. Remove from the heat and add the peanut butter, mixing until smooth.

4. Whisk the eggs in a small bowl, and pour into the chocolate mixture, whisking constantly until they are completely incorporated.

5. Add the flour and salt and mix until just blended.

6. Pour into the prepared pan.

7. Preheat the oven to 300°F (150°C). Place the pan with the batter in the freezer for 30 minutes while you prepare the Peanut Butter and Raisin Layer.

8. After the brownies have been in the freezer, spread the peanut butter layer evenly overtop.

9. Bake for 30 minutes. The brownies should still be soft at the center but firm at the edges. If not, bake for an additional 5 minutes.

10. Cool and serve at room temperature when the flavor is best—the bars remain chewy and decidedly decadent!

Peanut Butter and Raisin Layer:

1 cup (250 mL) peanut butter

3 Tbsp (45 g) butter at room temperature

¼ cup + 2 Tbsp (50 g) icing sugar

1 egg

1 cup (150 g) raisins

1. Beat the peanut butter, butter, icing sugar and egg together in a bowl until smooth.

2. Add the raisins and mix briefly.

PEANUT CARAMEL BROWNIES

YIELD: 24 BARS

Why didn't I think of these sooner? This is the brownie version of a Snickers bar, and for some reason I think my version is a lot, um, healthier! These are truly awesome, and come together in minutes if you have all the components. So have the components ready if you'd like to have these brownies on hand in the future (and believe me, after making these once, you will want them on hand): bake a brownie slab and freeze it; make the Caramel Butterscotch Sauce and keep it in the fridge; and prepare some ganache, which you should always have in the fridge anyway for the proverbial unannounced guests that show up at your door . . . although they've never darkened my doorstep . . . although maybe if they knew I had these on hand . . .

9- × 13-inch slab (23 × 33 cm) your favorite dense brownie, baked and thoroughly chilled (frozen is okay)

2 cups (240 g) salted, dry-roasted peanuts

¾ cup (185 mL) Caramel Butterscotch Sauce (see page 18)

¾ cup (185 mL) ganache (see page 13)

1. Place the brownie slab bottom side up in a parchment-lined pan, preferably the pan it was baked in so it sits snuggly (but not absolutely necessary).

2. Place the peanuts in a medium-sized bowl.

3. Place the Caramel Butterscotch Sauce in a separate small bowl and set it in a shallow pan of simmering water. Stir until it becomes runny.

4. Pour the caramel over the peanuts and stir with a rubber spatula until they are well coated.

5. Spread the peanuts as quickly as possibly in an even layer over the brownies, using a spatula. The caramel cools pretty quickly so you may have trouble spreading them. In this case, dampen your hands and gently tap and push the peanuts into areas that are still exposed. Let set about 30 minutes.

6. Place the ganache in a small bowl and heat until there are only a few lumps still visible Remove from the heat and stir gently until it is completely smooth and lump and bubble free.

7. Pour about three-quarters of the heated ganache in a big pool in the middle of the peanut-covered brownie slab. Pick up the pan and tilt it so that the ganache rolls over the far left side then the far right side, then tilt it towards you and away from you. Don't worry if you don't cover the entire slab as you have one-quarter of ganache left. When the ganache has cloaked most of the peanuts, pour the remaining ganache either in the center or in those areas which are exposed. Tilt as necessary to cover the peanuts as much as possible.

8. Let set for at least a half an hour and then chill before slicing. Lift out of the pan using the parchment paper "wings" and set it on a cutting board.

9. Slice using a chef's knife dipped in hot water and wipe it clean after every slice.

FLOURLESS BROWNIES

YIELD: 16 BARS

The Jewish holiday of Passover always poses baking challenges. No ordinary flour and absolutely no leavening agents, such as baking powder, soda or yeast, are allowed. Hence there are dozens of recipes for egg-leavened tortes, chiffon, and jelly-roll-type cakes. Most of these are what I would characterize as traditional cakes and don't elicit the oohs and aahs that spur contemporary bakers to create new and amazing recipes. So every Passover, I set out to create the most chocolaty flourless dessert possible. This is one of them. You certainly don't have to wait for Passover to serve these brownies and they're perfect for anyone with a gluten allergy.

2 oz (56 g) unsweetened chocolate, chopped

4 oz (113 g) bittersweet chocolate, chopped

1 cup (227 g) butter, in cubes

1 cup (200 g) sugar

1 Tbsp (15 mL) cocoa

1 Tbsp (15 mL) molasses

¾ tsp (4 mL) kosher salt

4 eggs, lightly beaten

4 oz (113 g) pecans, toasted and finely ground

4 oz (113 g) whole pecan pieces, toasted

1. Preheat the oven to 300°F (150°C). Grease an 8-inch (20 cm) square pan and line with overhanging parchment paper.

2. Place both chocolates and the butter, sugar, cocoa, molasses and salt in a medium saucepan over low heat.

3. Stir until the chocolate and butter are melted and the sugar, cocoa, and molasses are thoroughly blended. It's okay if the mixture is grainy with sugar.

4. Remove the pan from the heat and whisk in the eggs. The batter will be thick and glossy.

5. Add the 4 oz (112 g) of ground pecans and stir well.

6. Pour the batter into the prepared pan. Top with an even layer of whole pecans.

7. Bake for 30 minutes or until the edges are firm but the center is still jiggly.

8. Cool to room temperature and then refrigerate.

9. These brownies are incredible when still slightly warm, unstoppable when room temperature, and densely chewy and delicious when cold. They also last forever.

10. Cut into small pieces because they are rich!

BROWNIE POINTER

Toasted ground and whole almonds and ½ tsp (2 mL) of almond extract are a delicious substitute for the pecans.

JURASSIC BROWNIES

YIELD: 16 BARS

These are called Jurassic Brownies because when I first assembled them, the components were made sometime in the previous year, put into the freezer and then forgotten about . . . until it came time to once again clean out the freezer and challenge myself to come up with something amazing. The ingredients are layered and each bite excavates new and wonderful—not to mention surprising—flavors. These are reminiscent of Congo bars, aka 7-layer bars, and they use many, if not most, of the items in Chapter One: crumble, crème d'amande, rummed fruit, curd, nuts and caramel. If you have all of these in the freezer, after a bit of time to thaw, this recipe takes 10 minutes to assemble. If you don't, well, wait until you do! Chewy, gooey, crunchy and sweet, what more could one ask for?

12 oz (340 g) Rich Chocolate Crumble (see page 11)

12 oz (340 g) Crème d'Amande (see page 16)

12 oz (340 g) Rummed Raisins (or Rummed Dried Fruit) (see page 24)

12 oz (340 g) Brownie Curd (see page 8)

9 oz (250 g) Mocha-ed Nuts (see page 21)

2 Tbsp (30 mL) Caramel Butterscotch Sauce (see page 18)

1. Preheat the oven to 300°F (150°C). Line an 8-inch (20 cm) square pan with overhanging parchment paper. Grease the exposed sides with vegetable spray.

2. Press the crumble evenly into the pan.

3. Mix the Crème d'Amande until it's softened and spreadable. Spread evenly over the brownie layer.

4. Sprinkle the Rummed Raisins over the Crème d'Amande.

5. Warm the Brownie Curd over simmering water and whisk until it is smooth and shiny.

6. Spread over the fruit and make it an even layer.

7. Bake for 20 minutes. Remove from the oven and press the Mocha-ed Nuts evenly over the curd.

8. Bake an additional 8–10 minutes.

9. Remove from the oven and immediately drizzle the Caramel Butterscotch Sauce evenly over the top.

10. Cool completely in the pan, then chill in the fridge overnight before attempting to slice the brownies.

11. Lift the slab out of the pan by running a knife around the edges, using the parchment paper as handles.

Christopher Freeland

Jackson Pollock Bars

YIELD: 20 BARS

I love the traditional 7-layer bars, sometimes known as Congo bars, but as I get older, they've become too sweet for my taste. Here's my adult version with a finish that makes them look just like a Jackson Pollock canvas. You need Classic Brownie batter, Caramel Butterscotch Sauce and Ganache to complete them quickly. If you don't have graham cracker crumbs, but you do have some leftover chocolate cake or brownie crumbs, use them instead.

½ cup (115 g) butter

3 cups (750 mL) graham cracker crumbs

3 oz (85 g) whole hazelnuts, toasted and skinned

3 oz (85 g) hazelnuts, toasted, skinned and chopped

1 cup (100 g) toasted coconut

1 cup (250 mL) Classic Brownie batter (see page 29)

1 cup (250 mL) sweetened condensed milk

2 Tbsp (30 mL) finely chopped candied ginger

2½ oz (75 g) slivered almonds

¼ cup (60 mL) ganache (see page 13)

¼ cup (60 mL) Caramel Butterscotch Sauce (see page 18)

1. Preheat the oven to 300°F (150°C). Line a 9- × 13-inch (23 × 33 cm) pan with overhanging parchment paper.

2. Place the butter in a small saucepan over low heat and melt until it has turned a golden brown.

3. Mix with the graham cracker crumbs and press into the bottom of the prepared pan. It will be a fairly thin layer.

4. Bake in the oven for 15 minutes.

5. Remove from the oven and sprinkle with the whole hazelnuts, then the chopped hazelnuts on top.

6. Sprinkle the toasted coconut over the hazelnuts.

7. Mix the Classic Brownie batter with the sweetened condensed milk and drizzle over the coconut.

8. Distribute the ginger and the slivered almonds evenly on top.

9. Bake for about 25 minutes or until slightly bubbly on top. Don't overbake.

10. Remove from the oven and cool completely.

11. Warm both the ganache and the Caramel Butterscotch Sauce to the point where they are just pourable, about 80–85°F (27–30°C).

12. From a height of about 2 feet (60 cm), evenly drizzle first the ganache and then the caramel over the top to create a splattered, drizzled effect.

13. Let firm up before slicing into bars.

CHOCOLATE RASPBERRY PEANUT BUTTER CRUMBLE BARS

YIELD: 24 BARS

Some people fantasize about sex; me, I fantasize about brownies (sorry, Howard) and about how I can pack just about every flavor and texture I love into a single bar. These come pretty close to perfection, what with creamy peanut butter, rich, fudgy chocolate, the tang of raspberries and the crunch of crumble. Okay, so it's no substitute for sex, but it comes pretty close!

1 pint (150 g) raspberries

1 Tbsp (15 mL) sugar

2¾ cups (360 g) all-purpose flour

¼ cup (30 g) cocoa

1½ tsp (7 mL) baking soda

1½ tsp (7 mL) baking powder

½ tsp (2 mL) kosher salt

1 cup (227 g) butter

1 cup (250 mL) peanut butter

1 cup + 2 Tbsp (225 g) sugar

2 eggs

2 tsp (10 mL) vanilla extract

6 oz (170 g) chocolate, chopped

½ cup (125 mL) ganache (see page 13)

icing sugar for dusting

1. Preheat the oven to 350°F (180°C). Grease a 9- × 13-inch (23 × 33 cm) baking pan and line with overhanging parchment paper.

2. In a small saucepan, heat the raspberries and 1 Tbsp (15 mL) sugar until the raspberries become soft. Remove from the heat and cool. This is your raspberry purée.

3. Mix together the flour, cocoa, baking soda, baking powder and salt. Set aside.

4. In the bowl of an electric mixer, beat the butter and peanut butter together until smooth.

5. Add the sugar and beat until mixed, scraping the sides from time to time, about 2 minutes.

6. Add the eggs 1 at a time, scraping the sides of the bowl after each addition.

7. Add the vanilla and blend briefly.

8. Add the flour and cocoa mixture and mix only until blended.

9. Remove 1½ cups (375 mL) of batter from the bowl and place in a second bowl. Add the chocolate chips to the bowl and mix with a rubber spatula.

10. Press the batter without the chocolate chips into the prepared pan. Spread the raspberry purée on top.

11. Create a crumble topping by dropping the batter with the chocolate chips in little blobs evenly over the surface of the raspberry purée.

12. Bake for about 25–30 minutes, watching carefully that the crumble doesn't burn.

13. Remove from the oven and cool completely.

14. Drizzle with the ganache (warmed) and let set.

15. Dust with icing sugar and slice.

Inner Peace Caramel Brownies

YIELD: 16 BARS

These are pure flavor. The deep, thick chocolate batter is glossy going into the oven and stays that way until it's time to come out. These are major fudgy, to the point of being wet at the center. Cool in the fridge for an even fudgier texture. The darker the caramel, the edgier (slightly more bitter) the flavor. The first time around, don't go too dark, then be daring! They taste superb served warm with a scoop of vanilla ice cream.

1¾ cups (350 g) sugar

¼ cup (60 mL) water

½ cup (115 g) butter

¾ cup (150 g) sugar

4 oz (113 g) bittersweet chocolate, chopped

3 eggs

1 tsp (5 mL) vanilla extract

¼ tsp (1 mL) kosher salt

¾ cup (100 g) all-purpose flour

1. Set aside a bowl of ice water big enough to hold a 6-inch (15 cm) saucepan.

2. Place the sugar and water in the saucepan over medium heat.

3. Bring to a boil, stirring to dissolve the sugar. Use a pastry brush dipped in cold water to brush down any sugar crystals on the side of the pan, or cover the pan briefly so the steam created inside the pot can dissolve any crystals.

4. Boil the sugar until it starts to caramelize. Watch it carefully, because a few things happen. In some pans, caramelization will occur on one side of the pan before the other; in this instance, swirl the pot gently to get an even color. In other pans, once the sugar begins to brown, it goes from light to dark very quickly and will continue to cook even when removed from the heat. When the sugar has become a medium chestnut brown (it should really be brown, but not dark), remove from the heat and immediately set the bottom of the pan into the bowl of ice water. This will stop the cooking. If you don't think it's quite brown enough, remove it from the heat, watch it carefully and when it gets to the desired color, set it in the ice water.

5. Preheat the oven to 350°F (180°C). Line an 8-inch (20 cm) square pan with overhanging parchment paper.

6. In a medium saucepan, melt the butter with the sugar. Remove from the heat and add the chocolate. Stir until it is melted and the mixture is thick and glossy.

7. Add the cooled caramel mixture and mix thoroughly.

8. Break the eggs into a small bowl and whisk lightly. Add all at once to the chocolate mixture and whisk until smooth and glossy.

9. Add the vanilla and salt. Mix to blend.

10. Add the flour and mix only enough to blend.

11. Pour into the prepared pan and bake for 25–30 minutes.

12. Remove and cool completely.

Peanut Butter Brownie Bars

YIELD: 16 BARS

No matter how I try to stay away from the chocolate-nut combination, and the chocolate-peanut combination in particular, my mind keeps creating new ways to wed these two well-suited mates. The earthiness of peanuts contrasts with chocolate so that the flavors neither stand apart nor merge into one. It's truly a marriage made in heaven.

Brownie Bottom:

1 oz (28 g) unsweetened chocolate, chopped

5 oz (140 g) bittersweet chocolate, chopped

¼ cup + 2 Tbsp (90 mL) peanut butter at room temperature

4 Tbsp (55 g) butter at room temperature

½ cup (110 g) brown sugar

2 eggs

¼ cup (35 g) whole wheat flour

½ tsp (2 mL) kosher salt

6 oz (170 g) bittersweet chocolate, chopped

1 recipe Peanut Butter Topping

1 cup (250 mL) ganache (see page 13), liquid but cool

1. Preheat the oven to 300°F (150°C). Line an 8-inch (20 cm) square pan with overhanging parchment paper.

2. Place the chocolates in a microwaveable bowl. Microwave for 1 minute, check, stir and microwave again for about 1 more minute, being careful to not burn the chocolate.

3. In the bowl of an electric mixer, beat the peanut butter and butter until soft.

4. Add the sugar and beat until blended.

5. Add the melted chocolate, mixing for about 1 minute and scraping the bottom and sides of the bowl from time to time.

6. Add the eggs, mixing to blend.

7. Whisk together the flour and salt.

8. Add to the bowl and mix on low speed for about 1 minute.

9. Fold in the chopped chocolate. The batter will be thick.

10. Spread into the prepared pan and bake for about 25–30 minutes. The brownie will feel soft to the touch but will firm up as it cools. Cool completely.

11. Spread Peanut Butter Topping over the cooled brownies. Place in the refrigerator to set.

12. Pour the ganache over the brownie slab. Tilt the rack in a circular motion to spread the ganache. Let set.

13. Place the brownie slab on a cutting board. Cut with a thin knife, heating it under hot water and drying it between each slice.

14. Store tightly covered in the fridge for up to 3 weeks.

¾ cup (185 mL) peanut butter

½ cup (115 g) butter

½ cup (60 g) icing sugar

½ tsp (2 mL) ground cardamom

¼ tsp (1 mL) kosher salt

Peanut But

Place all the ingr

BROWN

There are s
it would be
Hazelnut ar
¾ tsp (4 mL)
a more pron

ter Topping:

dients in the bowl of a food processor. Process until smooth.

> **IE POINTER**
>
> many nut butters on the market these days that
> a shame to make these only with peanut butter.
> l almond butter would be delicious, too—but add
> lmond extract to the brownie batter with the eggs for
> unced almond flavor.

10. When the cookie bites are completely cool, carefully fold them into the brownie batter, taking care not to overmix and break them up. You want them to stay in their original shape.

11. Pour the batter into the prepared pan and gently smooth the top.

12. Crumble the remaining one-third of the dough evenly between your fingers over the brownie batter to create a nice crunchy topping.

13. Bake for 25–30 minutes. The batter shouldn't jiggle, but it shouldn't be puffed up. either. The crumble will be golden brown on top and firm.

14. Remove from the oven and cool completely in the pan. Lift out of the pan holding both sides of the parchment paper.

15. When completely cool, dust the top with icing sugar.

16. Cut into slices with a wet knife, wiping it clean after every slice.

17. Store tightly covered in the fridge for up to a week. The crumble will get less crunchy over time.

No Bake Brownies

YIELD: 24 BARS

I don't know whether these are brownies or candy, but whichever they are, they're hard to beat in both taste and ease of preparation. The next time you need something to impress the boss or win kudos at the bake sale, bring these!

7 oz (200 g) bittersweet chocolate, chopped

1 lb (454 g) milk chocolate, chopped

4 Tbsp (55 g) butter

10 marshmallows

¾ cup (175 mL) corn syrup

2 cups (500 mL) peanut butter

½ cup (110 g) brown sugar

4 oz (113 g) peanuts, chopped

3 cups (100 g) crispy rice cereal

1 cup (250 mL) ganache (optional, page 13)

1. Line a 9- × 13-inch (23 × 33 cm) pan with overhanging parchment paper.

2. In a large, heavy saucepan over medium-low heat, melt both chocolates and the butter.

3. Add the marshmallows. Stir until the marshmallows and chocolate are completely melted.

4. Remove from the heat and stir in the corn syrup, peanut butter and brown sugar. Mix until smooth, about 1 minute.

5. Add the peanuts and rice cereal, mixing lightly but thoroughly.

6. Pour into the prepared pan and smooth with a spatula.

7. Let set or place in the fridge to firm up.

8. If you are glazing the bars, warm the ganache until pourable, about 80–85°F (27–30°C). Pour it in a steady stream over the center of the brownie slab in the pan. It will spread out towards the sides in a circular pattern.

9. Lift the pan and tilt from side to side until the entire surface is covered with a smooth and glossy glaze. Cool completely.

10. To remove from the pan, wet a sponge under hot water and press it against the sides of the brownie pan. You will see the glaze melt around the edges as you move the sponge along the sides.

11. Gently lift the slab by the overhanging parchment and place it on a cutting board to slice.

12. Store in the fridge, well wrapped, for 3 weeks or in the freezer for 3 months.

Here's an even faster version. Melt both chocolates. While they're melting, in a large bowl, combine the peanuts (or any other nut, for that matter), 1 cup (120 g) raisins (or any other dried fruit cut to the same size as a raisin), crispy rice cereal (or substitute a bran cereal for something a tad healthier), and the marshmallows cut into pieces the size of raisins. Pour in the melted chocolate and mix gently with a rubber spatula, coating everything with the chocolate. To complete you have two options: either drop by tablespoons onto a parchment-lined baking sheet and let cool completely or press into a 9- × 13-inch (23 × 33 cm) parchment-lined pan and cut into bars before the chocolate has solidified completely. Store in a tightly sealed container for about a week.

OOZY WALNUT BARS

YIELD: 24 BARS

I love pecan pie but it needs chocolate! In this recipe, I've added chocolate in the form of Mascarpone Chocolate Curd—just in case there wasn't enough richness for you—and used walnuts instead of pecans for their slight bitterness. Good walnuts are hard to find. Bad ones, alas, are not only easy to pick up everywhere, but they also destroy anything you put them in, so taste before you buy. Don't be frugal. Buy good California walnuts or risk spoiling this fabulous bittersweet filling. The baking method is, to say the least, unorthodox and resulted when I started the recipe only to realize I had to be at work in 10 minutes. So I turned the oven off after 10 minutes baking and returned at the end of the day to perfectly oozy bars. If you want to bake them to the end, bake for no longer than 20 minutes; otherwise, just let the warmth of the oven do its job while you go out to do yours!

11 oz (310 g) unbaked Pâte Sucrée au Chocolat (see page 5) pastry dough

1 cup (250 mL) Mascarpone Chocolate Curd (see page 10)

½ cup (110 g) brown sugar

½ cup (125 mL) corn syrup

2 eggs

½ tsp (2 mL) kosher salt

12 oz (340 g) whole walnuts or large pieces

1. Preheat the oven to 350°F (180°C). Line a 9- × 13-inch (23 × 33 cm) pan with overhanging parchment paper.

2. Press the Pâte Sucrée au Chocolat into the prepared pan in an even but thin layer. Refrigerate 10 minutes.

3. Bake for 10 minutes.

4. While the crust is baking, whisk together the curd, sugar, corn syrup, eggs and salt.

5. Remove the crust from the oven. Pour the filling over the crust and sprinkle with the nuts.

6. Place in the oven and set the timer for 10 minutes.

7. After 10 minutes, turn the oven off and let the residual heat of the oven finish the baking. After an hour, you can remove the pan.

8. Let cool completely before cutting into squares.

> ### BROWNIE POINTERS
>
> - These bars, with their thin crust, are fragile when still warm and may crumble when sliced. For easier slicing, chill completely, then let come to room temperature before serving.
>
> - For Boozy Walnut Bars, add 2 Tbsp (30 mL) bourbon whisky to the eggs before mixing with the Mascarpone Chocolate Curd.

LISA AND JIM'S "HERE IS WHAT I DID" CHOCOLATE OATMEAL BROWNIES

YIELD: 24 BARS

Jim is a dear friend and confidant at work. We laugh a lot together and share recipes. This is one that he adapted from a recipe from his sister, who in turn got it years ago from a women's magazine. Jim quadrupled the recipe and replaced the shortening with butter. And I've substituted whole wheat flour for the all-purpose, reduced the quantity a bit and replaced the cocoa with chocolate chips. Feel free to adapt this recipe as your own. Melt some of the chocolate chips and mix them into the batter. You can also add toasted walnuts; they add a great crunch and depth of flavor.

1 lb (454 g) butter at room temperature

2 cups (440 g) brown sugar

1 cup (200 g) granulated sugar

4 eggs

2 Tbsp (30 mL) vanilla extract

4 cups (400 g) quick cooking oats

3 cups (390 g) whole wheat flour

2 tsp (10 mL) kosher salt

2 tsp (10 mL) baking soda

1 lb (454 g) chocolate chips

1. Preheat the oven to 300°F (150°C).

2. In the bowl of an electric mixer, beat the butter and sugars until mixed but not fluffy.

3. Add the eggs and vanilla and beat for 1 minute, scraping down the sides and bottom.

4. Add the oats, flour, salt, baking soda and chocolate chips, turning the mixer on and off in quick succession so you don't have flour flying all over the kitchen. Once the batter is moistened, don't mix any more than is necessary. (Now would be the time to add that melted chocolate mentioned in the recipe introduction, if you so choose.)

5. Dump the dough onto a 9- × 18-inch (23 × 45 cm) jellyroll pan lined with parchment paper. Spread out and flatten to fill pan.

6. Bake for about 20 minutes until firm around the edges but still soft in the middle.

7. Cool for about 15 minutes before cutting into squares.

8. Store in an airtight container. These have a short shelf life.

BROWNIE POINTER

The first time I made these, I stuffed the batter into a 9-inch (23 cm) square pan, which was too small. The batter went right to the brim and it took forever to bake; indeed, I left the house with my automatic oven set to turn itself off at the end of the baking time. My husband forgot that they were in the oven so they continued to bake as the oven cooled. By the time they were removed from the oven they were pretty solid. As I am not one to throw anything away, I cut the slab into quarters and then sliced each quarter into biscotti slices. The slices went into the oven again until they crisped. I brought them for my friends at work, my toughest critics: they loved them! So if you want to duplicate the recipe, bake in a 9-inch (23 cm) square pan. Baking time will be 45 minutes to an hour, until the center no longer feels soft; indeed it will feel quite firm (but not hard as rock). Cool and cut into ¼-inch (6 mm) slices. Place in a 300°C (150°C) oven for 15 minutes.

CRANBERRY WALNUT CHOCOLATE CHIP BLONDIES

YIELD: 16 BARS/56 (YES, 56!) CUBES. IT'S SO RICH, 1 OR 2 CUBES ARE ALL MANY PEOPLE WILL NEED.

These started out as my Raspberry Blondies, but a foray down to the freezer revealed no raspberries but Yes!—frozen cranberries and a bag of recently toasted walnuts. And I had a happy accident: I was busy making another recipe while melting the butter, and it went a little bit too far in the pan. It cooked to a wonderful nutty brown—i.e., I inadvertently made browned butter, which has a wonderful flavor! And because the butter was so hot, the chocolate chunks started to melt, so it wasn't really blondies in the end but an incredibly amazing "almost brownie," with a sweet but tart kiss.

¾ cup (170 g) butter

1¾ cups (385 g) brown sugar

2 eggs

1 Tbsp (15 mL) maple syrup

1 tsp (5 mL) vanilla extract

1¾ cups (225 g) whole wheat flour

½ tsp (2 mL) kosher salt

4¼ oz (120 g) toasted walnuts, coarsely chopped

6 oz (170 g) bittersweet chocolate, coarsely chopped in the food processor

2 cups (180 mL) fresh or frozen cranberries, pulsed in a food processor

1. Preheat the oven to 300°F (150°C). Line a 9-inch (23 cm) square pan with overhanging parchment paper. Grease the exposed sides with vegetable spray.

2. Place the butter in a large saucepan over medium heat. Cook until it foams, browns and then ceases to foam, but be careful that it doesn't burn. Remove from the heat and cool for about 10 minutes.

3. Stir in the brown sugar. It will be a thick mass. Cool for an additional 5 minutes.

4. Stir in the eggs, whisking quickly until smooth.

5. Add the maple syrup and vanilla. Mix to blend.

6. Add the flour and salt and combine. The batter will now be fairly thick.

7. Add the nuts, chocolate and cranberries, stirring until incorporated.

8. Spread the dough in the prepared pan.

9. Bake for about 35 minutes or until the center is slightly puffed. It will be soft but not wiggly to the touch.

10. Remove from the oven and cool on a wire rack in the pan.

11. Chill completely before slicing.

Triple Espresso Brownies

YIELD: 24 BARS

I grew up in the coffee business and started drinking coffee at age 12 when I read an article in the New York Times that said coffee consumption was down. I thought my entry into the market would be good for my dad's business. Little did I know that years later I'd be running Canada's second-largest coffee company! Coffee and chocolate are one of those food combinations that go together because they grow together. They share a similar but not identical terroir, or geography. This brownie adds a twist of lemon to the filling, just like an Italian espresso. Don't substitute instant coffee for the real thing here. Start the ganache, then make the cream cheese filling and finally the batter. This makes enough for a crowd.

Espresso Ganache:

10 oz (280 g) bittersweet chocolate, chopped

7 oz (200 g) white chocolate, chopped

1 cup (250 mL) whipping cream

1 Tbsp (15 mL) freshly ground espresso powder

pinch kosher salt

1. Place both chocolates in a bowl.

2. Place the cream and espresso powder in a small saucepan set over medium heat. Bring to just below the boil, when bubbles appear around the edges of the surface.

3. Remove from the heat and let steep while you make the cream cheese filling and the brownies.

4. When the brownies are in the oven, finish the ganache by reheating the cream to just below the boil.

5. Pour over the chopped chocolates and let sit for 5 minutes. Whisk until smooth. Whisk in the salt.

6. Set aside until the brownies are ready for glazing.

Lemon Cream Cheese Filling:

8 oz (227 g) cream cheese

1 lemon, grated rind of

2 Tbsp (30 mL) lemon juice

¼ cup (50 g) sugar

2 eggs

1. Place all the ingredients in the bowl of a food processor and whip until smooth.

2. Pour into a bowl and set aside while you prepare the brownies.

9 oz (255 g) bittersweet chocolate, chopped

2 oz (56 g) unsweetened chocolate, chopped

¾ cup (170 g) butter

2 cups (400 g) sugar

4 Tbsp (60 mL) freshly ground espresso powder, divided

4 eggs

½ cup (65 g) all-purpose flour

pinch kosher salt

Triple Espresso Brownie Batter:

1. Preheat the oven to 300°F (150°C). Line a 9- × 13-inch (23 × 33 cm) baking pan with overhanging parchment paper.

2. Place both chocolates in a medium-sized bowl over a pot of simmering water.

3. Add the butter and whisk from time to time until smooth and completely melted.

4. Add the sugar and 2 Tbsp (30 mL) of the espresso powder. Whisk to blend. It will be granular in appearance.

5. Remove from the heat. Cool 10 minutes.

6. Whisk in the eggs 1 at a time. Because the batter is still warm, it is important to whisk quickly. Adding the eggs will thicken the batter.

7. Whisk in the flour and salt, mixing only enough to blend well.

8. Pour half the batter into the prepared pan. Drizzle half the cream cheese filling over the batter base. Spoon the remaining brownie batter over the cream cheese filling and spread gently to the corners, covering the cream cheese. Drizzle the remaining cream cheese filling over the batter. It may sink. Don't worry.

9. Bake for 30 minutes. The brownie will appear puffed and jiggly.

10. Remove from the oven. Let it cool for about an hour.

11. Pour the prepared ganache on top and sprinkle with the remaining 2 Tbsp (30 mL) espresso powder.

12. Place in the fridge to cool completely.

13. Use the parchment paper to lift out the brownie slab and slice.

Bitter Bitter Chocolate Brownies
(aka Jimbo's 80th Birthday "Cake")

YIELD: 16 BARS

My dad and I used to see the New York Giants when they played at Yankee Stadium. I loved being with him, and I loved the great hot dogs we'd get at a deli underneath the "El" (elevated subway) and the chocolate bars that would crack when we ate them because it was so cold outside. To this day, my dad loves chocolate, so there was nothing more fitting than this dessert for his 80th birthday, celebrated among family and friends. There's a high percentage of bitter chocolate relative to the amount of sugar—I wanted to make an "adult" brownie with a deep chocolate flavor. At first the taste is surprisingly bitter, but as it warms in your mouth (or if you eat it warm) the true essence of chocolate comes to the fore. These are superb with vanilla ice cream.

6½ oz (185 g) unsweetened chocolate

½ cup (115 g) butter

¾ cup (150 g) sugar

3 eggs

1 Tbsp (15 mL) vanilla extract

1 Tbsp (15 mL) instant coffee granules

¼ tsp (1 mL) kosher salt

½ cup (65 g) all-purpose flour

1. Preheat the oven to 300°F (150°C). Line an 8-inch (20 cm) square pan with parchment paper.

2. In a medium saucepan, melt the chocolate and butter.

3. Add the sugar and stir over very low heat until it is almost all dissolved, about 10 minutes.

4. Remove from the heat and cool for about 10 minutes before adding the eggs.

5. Whisk the eggs with the vanilla and gradually add to the chocolate mixture, stirring constantly so they don't cook.

6. Add the instant coffee and salt and mix well.

7. Stir in the flour, blending until just incorporated.

8. Pour into the prepared pan and bake for 30 minutes.

9. Remove from the oven and serve warm with vanilla ice cream and nothing else!

CARAMEL GANACHE BITTERSWEET BROWNIES

YIELD: 16 BARS

Who says there can be too much of a good thing? Certainly not me. The Bitter Bitter Chocolate Brownies (facing page) enter the pantheon of the sublime with the layering of caramel, ganache and toasted pecans and a sprinkling of salt. After consuming just a few bites, your life will never be the same again.

1 recipe baked, chilled Bitter Bitter Chocolate Brownies (previous page), in the pan

½ cup (125 mL) Caramel Butterscotch Sauce (see page 18)

½ cup (125 mL) ganache (see page 13)

16 toasted pecans (optional)

sea salt (optional)

1. Spread the Caramel Butterscotch Sauce over the top of the chilled brownie.

2. Place in the freezer for 30 minutes.

3. Warm the ganache to the point where it is just pourable and barely warm to the touch, about 80–85°F (27–30°C).

4. Remove the brownies from the freezer and pour the ganache in a pool in the center of the pan. Quickly spread the chocolate to the edges in as few strokes as possible.

5. Top with the toasted pecans, if using, placed in 4 × 4 rows so each bar gets a pecan.

6. Sprinkle very lightly with fine sea salt, if desired.

7. Slice and serve!

RASPBERRY BROWNIES

YIELD: 16 BARS

*Yum! That is almost all I can say about these brownies. Dense, fudgy
and intense with real raspberry flavor.*

1 pint (150 g) fresh raspberries

1 Tbsp (15 mL) granulated sugar

8 oz (227 g) unsweetened chocolate

1 cup (227 g) butter

2 cups (400 g) granulated sugar

½ cup (110 g) brown sugar

4 eggs

⅛ tsp (0.5 mL) kosher salt

½ cup (65 g) all-purpose flour

1½ cups (325 mL) ganache
  (see page 13)

> **BROWNIE POINTER**
>
> Top each brownie with a fresh
> raspberry.

1. To make the raspberry purée, place the raspberries and the 1 Tbsp (15 mL) sugar in a small saucepan. Add 1 Tbsp (15 mL) of water and place over low heat. Mash the raspberries with a wooden spoon or rubber spatula.

2. Bring to a boil, then lower the heat. Cook until you have a thickened sauce. Be careful it doesn't burn!

3. Place mixture in a sieve and press it through with a spatula. You should have about 1 cup (250 mL) of seedless purée.

4. Preheat the oven to 300°F (150°C). Line a 9-inch (23 cm) square pan with parchment paper.

5. Melt the chocolate and butter over low heat. Blend well.

6. Add the 2 cups (400 g) granulated sugar and the brown sugar. Mix until both are almost completely dissolved.

7. Add the eggs 1 at a time, beating until completely smooth and glossy.

8. Add the salt and half the raspberry purée. Blend well.

9. Add the flour and mix just enough to blend.

10. Pour into the prepared pan and bake for 30 minutes.

11. Remove from the oven and cool completely.

12. If necessary, warm the ganache in the microwave on medium power or over barely boiling water until just melted, about 80–85°F (27–30°C).

13. Add the remaining raspberry purée to the ganache and whisk until smooth.

14. Pour mixture over the brownies and tilt the pan to spread the ganache smoothly.

15. Let sit until the glaze is set. Cut and serve!

APPLE BUTTER BROWNIES

YIELD: 24 BARS

Apples and chocolate are amongst my two favorite foods, and I have long tried to combine them but with no success . . . until now. Apple butter has pectin, the ingredient that holds many jellies together, and therefore apple butter has the consistency of soft butter. It also has a wonderful caramel sweetness. In this recipe, I simply removed the butter to see what would happen. Whenever butter is removed from a recipe, a significant amount of flavor is lost along with the fat. In this case, however, the rich mouthfeel of the apple butter fills in wonderfully for the butter, as well as supplying a nice tang and a perfect, fudgy texture. My husband couldn't even tell that the butter had been removed!

10 oz (280 g) 70% bittersweet chocolate

1⅓ cups (265 g) sugar

1 cup (250 mL) apple butter, homemade or store-bought

5 eggs

1 tsp (5 mL) vanilla extract

3 Tbsp (25 g) whole wheat flour

3 cups (600 g) toasted pecan pieces

¼ cup (65 g) Caramel Butterscotch Sauce (see page 18)

pinch kosher salt

1. Preheat the oven to 300°F (150°C). Line an 8-inch (20 cm) square pan with 1 sheet of parchment paper overhanging 2 sides so you have "handles" to lift the baked slab out of the pan. Grease the exposed sides.

2. Place the chocolate in a large bowl over a pot of simmering water.

3. When it has melted partway, add the sugar. Stir with a rubber spatula until the chocolate is completely melted. Remove bowl from the pot.

4. In a small bowl whisk together the apple butter, eggs and vanilla.

5. Add to the chocolate mixture and blend until completely smooth.

6. Add the flour and mix only until blended.

7. Set aside 1 cup (200 g) of nuts and fold the rest into the batter.

8. Pour the batter into the prepared pan. Sprinkle the remaining nuts on top and press lightly so that they stick to the batter.

9. Bake for 20 minutes, no longer. Remove from the oven.

10. While still warm in the pan, drizzle the Caramel Butterscotch Sauce over the nuts.

11. Sprinkle the pinch of salt over the caramel.

12. Cool to room temperature and lift the slab out of the pan.

Brownies Forte

YIELD: 16 THICK SLICES

The Italians have their panforte and we have our holiday fruitcake. I've never heard jokes about the former but there may well be websites devoted to nonedible uses for the latter! Still, there really is nothing as luscious as a well-made fruitcake . . . unless of course, it's a chocolate version. So, taking my cue from the Italians, I offer you a wonderful new holiday classic also to become one of your favorite recipes year-round. Serve it ice-cold and thinly sliced alongside Gorgonzola or Roquefort cheese for a sophisticated, Continental dessert. Or, make it in early December, wrap in cellophane and a pretty ribbon and give it as a gift.

1 cup (150 g) golden raisins

¾ cup (100 g) dried cranberries

2½ oz (75 g) (about 12) dried apricots, diced

½ cup (115 g) prunes, diced

½ cup (70 g) dates, diced (about 20 small dates, pitted)

½ cup (70 g) dried figs, diced

¼ cup (35 g) high-quality candied citrus peel, diced

¼ cup (60 mL) rum

3½ oz (100 g) toasted hazelnuts

2 oz (56 g) whole unblanched almonds

1 Tbsp (15 mL) fennel seeds

½ cup (115 g) butter

1¼ cups (250 g) sugar

7 oz (200 g) bittersweet chocolate, chopped

¼ cup (60 mL) honey

1. Toss together the dried fruits with the rum. Let sit for 24 hours. (Or, if you don't have time, heat the rum over a low heat and remove before it begins to boil. Pour over the fruits and let sit until absorbed, about 1 hour.)

2. Preheat the oven to 300°F (150°C). Line a 9-inch (23 cm) square pan with overhanging parchment paper and grease the unlined sides.

3. Toss the nuts and fennel seeds together with the fruits.

4. In a medium saucepan over medium heat, melt the butter.

5. Add the sugar and stir until well mixed and the sugar has dissolved. The mixture will be smooth.

6. Turn off the heat and blend in the chocolate. Let sit for a minute or 2. Stir until completely smooth.

7. Add the honey and the almond extract.

8. Whisk together the eggs and gradually stir them into the chocolate. Whisk until shiny and smooth.

9. Add the flour and salt. Mix only until blended.

10. Pour the brownie batter over the dried fruits and nuts. Mix to coat well.

11. Pour into the prepared pan and spread with a spatula.

12. Bake for 1 hour, watching carefully that the sides do not burn. If they start to darken, turn down the heat to 275°F and cover the pan with foil.

13. Remove the brownies from the oven and immediately brush with the rum, allowing it to soak in before you brush some more.

¾ tsp (4 mL) almond extract

3 eggs

½ cup (65 g) instant flour (see page
vi) or all-purpose flour

½ tsp (2 mL) kosher salt

¼ cup (60 mL) rum for brushing

14. Cool. Lift the brownies out of the pan using the parchment wings.
To serve, cut into 16 slices, or as thinly as you wish.

15. Wrapped tightly in plastic and, refrigerated, these brownies have a
lcooong shelf life.

BROWNIE POINTERS

- A beautiful variation is to omit the rum bath after the brownies
come out of the oven and instead brush the top with some apri-
cot jam that you have warmed and sieved. Sprinkle the jam with
an even layer of toasted pine nuts.

- You can vary the proportions of dried fruits, or substitute any
of your favorite dried fruits, with a total measurement of 4 cups
(approximately 600 g). For an extra dimension of flavor, add 2 oz
(56 g) diced candied ginger.

- If you don't have rum to macerate the fruits, brandy, kirsch or
other fruit liqueur would be delightful alternatives.

REALLY FUDGY NONDAIRY BROWNIES

YIELD: 24 INCREDIBLY MOIST AND CHOCOLATE-LADEN BROWNIE CUBES

Every Jewish holiday we invite new guests to join our celebration. And every year there's a new dietary restriction: some of us are getting older and are cholesterol challenged; others are getting to an age where meat just doesn't cut it anymore; still others have become lactose intolerant. Oy! What's a cook to do? This year it was someone who was strictly kosher, meaning that we couldn't serve dairy if we were serving meat, which we were. So the desserts, and especially the brownies, had to be dairy free. Most nondairy desserts taste (to me) overwhelmingly of the oil that is used in place of real butter. Not these babies. Everyone raved. You will too, of course. The Coffee Glaze is amazing, too, adding another dimension of chocolate. You could make these by substituting melted butter for the oil but of course they wouldn't be nondairy any more.

½ cup (125 mL) grapeseed oil

2 Tbsp (30 mL) walnut oil

1¾ cups (385 g) brown sugar

¾ cup (85 g) cocoa

⅔ cup (150 mL) brewed coffee

12 oz (340 g) bittersweet chocolate, chopped in chunks

3 eggs

2 tsp (10 mL) vanilla extract

½ tsp (2 mL) kosher salt

½ cup + 2 Tbsp (80 g) whole wheat flour

6½ oz (185 g) walnuts, coarsely chopped (optional)

1 recipe Coffee Glaze (optional)

1. Preheat the oven to 300°F (150°C). Line an 8-inch (20 cm) square pan with parchment paper and grease the sides with vegetable spray.

2. In a medium-sized saucepan, whisk the oils and brown sugar together. It will be a thick paste. Stir over medium heat until you can smell the walnut oil. Don't let it boil. Remove from the heat.

3. In a small bowl, whisk together the cocoa and the coffee until it is a smooth paste.

4. Add this to the sugar and oil mixture. It may sizzle and separate but with vigorous whisking it will come together again. Some sugar may stick to the bottom of the pan, but keep mixing. Don't worry about all of the sugar dissolving.

5. Add half of the chocolate chunks and mix until they melt. The mixture will be thick and smooth. Let sit for about 10 minutes to cool.

6. Whisk the eggs, vanilla and salt together in a small bowl and slowly add this to the chocolate mixture. Whisk until smooth.

7. Add the flour and whisk only until blended.

8. Add the rest of the chocolate chunks to the batter by folding them in gently.

9. Pour the batter into the prepared pan and spread evenly. Top evenly with the walnuts, if using.

10. Bake about 40 minutes or until the center no longer seems liquid beneath the surface. It will still be soft to the touch even though the edges will be firm.

11. Remove from the oven. Cool and chill completely because "really fudgy" in the title means "soft and gooey," i.e., refrigeration is a must.

12. Prepare the Coffee Glaze, if using, and spread over the chilled brownies. Let set.

13. Cut the brownies into cubes. Because the center is very gooey, wet your knife every time you make a cut. It's a nuisance but every slice will look professional.

Coffee Glaze:

4 oz (113 g) bittersweet chocolate, chopped

½ cup (115 g) vegetable shortening

¼ cup (60 mL) strong brewed coffee

pinch kosher salt

1. Place all the ingredients in a metal bowl.

2. Place in a pan of simmering water.

3. Whisk until smooth and there are no lumps of fat or chocolate.

BROWNIE POINTER

To adapt these for Passover, simply substitute matzoh flour for the all-purpose flour.

Gluten-Free Brownies

YIELD: 24 ONE-BITE BROWNIES

When making your first foray into gluten-free baking, this is a good place to start. Brownies don't need much to hold them together—in fact, you could do without the flour altogether (see my Flourless Brownies on page 50). Still, the texture differs without flour, and most gluten-free baking has a kind of sandy texture to it, usually thanks to rice flour. Not these. Between the cocoa nibs and the toasted walnuts crushed to the same size, you won't notice the rice and potato flours at all as long as you don't overbake the brownies. They should be soft to the touch in the center when you remove them from the oven. But if you do overbake them a bit, don't worry—glaze it with ganache and no one will notice.

½ cup (115 g) butter

3 Tbsp (45 mL) coconut oil or walnut oil

¾ cup (165 g) brown sugar

½ cup (100 g) granulated sugar

½ cup (55 g) cocoa

4 oz (113 g) bittersweet chocolate, chopped

3 eggs, lightly beaten

1 Tbsp (15 mL) brewed coffee

2 tsp (10 mL) vanilla extract

3 Tbsp (45 mL) rice flour

2 Tbsp (30 mL) potato flour

1 Tbsp (15 mL) potato starch

½ tsp (2 mL) cinnamon

1 tsp (5 mL) kosher salt

¼ cup (30 g) cocoa nibs (see Brownie Pointer on page 45)

2 oz (56 g) toasted walnuts crushed to the size of cocoa nibs

1. Preheat the oven to 300°F (150°C). Line an 8-inch (20 cm) square brownie pan with overhanging parchment paper.

2. Place the butter and the coconut oil in a saucepan over medium heat.

3. When they are almost fully melted, add the sugars and stir.

4. Add the cocoa, stir until smooth and remove from the heat.

5. Add the chocolate and stir well.

6. Whisk in the eggs vigorously, and then add the coffee and vanilla. The batter will feel sloshy and loose at first, but continued whisking will make it less so. It will come together in a smooth and almost shiny mass.

7. Add the rice flour, potato flour and starch, cinnamon and salt. Stir briefly until smooth.

8. Add the cocoa nibs and walnuts. Mix to incorporate and spread smoothly in the prepared pan.

9. Bake for 20 minutes. Cool brownies in the pan.

BUTTER- AND OIL-FREE OMEGA-3 BROWNIES

YIELD: 16 BARS

Every time an ingredient is added to a chocolate dessert, you risk diminishing the essence of the chocolate. Except for butter! There's no question that adding butter to brownies adds a depth of flavor that makes butter-free brownies, well, entirely different—but not always unpleasant. It was, however, a challenge for me to create a brownie that was healthier without sacrificing any of a brownie's essential being (or should I say its reason for being), which is: fudginess. This is that recipe. With a bit of whole wheat flour and some ground flaxseeds for an Omega-3 boost, you can feel good about eating a brownie made entirely without added butter . . . just don't overbake them!

¾ cup (150 g) granulated sugar

½ cup (110 g) brown sugar

⅓ cup (80 mL) brewed coffee

3½ oz (100 g) unsweetened chocolate

3½ oz (100 g) bittersweet chocolate

3 eggs

2 tsp (10 mL) vanilla extract

½ tsp (2 mL) kosher salt

3 Tbsp (45 mL) ground flaxseeds

¼ cup (35 g) whole wheat flour

1. Preheat the oven to 300°F (150°C). Line an 8-inch (20 cm) square pan with overhanging parchment paper and grease the exposed sides with vegetable spray.

2. Place the sugars and coffee in a deep saucepan.

3. Over medium heat, stir to dissolve the sugar and bring the mixture to a boil.

4. Remove from the heat, and add the chocolates. Whisk until smooth.

5. Add the eggs, 1 at a time, whisking until smooth.

6. Add the vanilla and salt.

7. Whisk in the ground flaxseeds and whole wheat flour.

8. Pour into the prepared pan and tilt or spread to make even.

9. Bake in the oven for about 20 minutes. The top will puff and be shiny.

10. Remove from the oven, and cool the brownies in the pan. Chill them further in the fridge so that they are easier to cut.

11. Flip the brownies onto a cutting board, and cut into squares. They will be fudgy and delicious.

VEGAN BROWNIES WITH COCOA NIBS AND SESAME SEEDS

YIELD: 16 BARS

How much can you remove from a brownie and still have it taste great? You're about to be surprised. The modern supermarket is full of wonderful substitutes that, with the exception of the shortening, one can easily call natural. And if you don't want to use the shortening, just substitute an equal amount of coconut oil. Between the cocoa nibs, toasted sesame seeds, dark coffee and cinnamon— not to mention the chocolate!—no one will be able to tell that the secret ingredient is tofu.

2 Tbsp (30 mL) coconut oil

2 Tbsp (30 mL) nonhydrogenated shortening

7 oz (200 g) bittersweet chocolate, chopped

3½ oz (100 g) unsweetened chocolate, chopped

one 10½ oz (300 g) package soft tofu

1¼ cups (275 g) brown sugar

1 Tbsp (15 mL) strong-brewed or espresso coffee

1 tsp (5 mL) vanilla extract

½ tsp (2 mL) kosher salt

½ cup (65 g) whole wheat flour

1 tsp (5 mL) cinnamon

2 Tbsp (30 mL) cocoa nibs (see Brownie Pointer on page 45)

2 Tbsp (30 mL) natural sesame seeds, toasted

1. Preheat the oven to 300°F (150°C). Line a 9-inch (23 cm) square pan with parchment paper and grease the sides with vegetable spray.

2. Place the 2 fats in a medium-sized saucepan over low heat. When they are partially melted, add the chocolates.

3. When most of the chocolate is melted remove the pan from the heat.

4. Place the tofu in the bowl of a food processor fitted with the steel blade.

5. Add the brown sugar, coffee, vanilla and salt. With the motor running, pour the chocolate mixture through the feed tube and process until the batter is completely smooth.

6. Stop the machine and add the flour and cinnamon. Pulse until it has disappeared into the batter.

7. Pour the batter into the prepared pan.

8. Sprinkle the cocoa nibs on top and press gently into the batter. Do the same with the sesame seeds, without entirely covering the whole surface. You may have some left over.

9. Bake for 35 minutes or until the sides are puffed and the center puffs slightly.

10. Cool, chill and slice.

CHAPTER 3

Deep, Dark and Delicious
Brownie Cakes

CHOCOLATE BROWNIE CRUMB CAKE

YIELD: 16 SERVINGS

My all-time favorite New York City specialty is crumb cake. All over the city, bakeries produce this great, simple cake from scratch. It's not always good, but in the Chelsea Market there's a bakery that makes the best there is. Its crumb layer is a good two times the height of the cake layer. The crumbs are pea-sized and crispy crunchy without being too tough or too sweet. The cake layer is a moist golden yellow cake, also not too sweet or too bland. An apple version that adds cinnamon to the crumbs and sautéed apples to the top of the cake below the crumbs just knocks my socks off. So, naturally, when thinking, nay dreaming, of a better version, I decided to make a chocolate brownie rendition. As I was editing this book, I visited the Chelsea Market and to my delight they had read my mind: what was missing was a chocolate crumb cake, and now they have it. Here's my version that's pretty darn close to the original.

1 recipe Rich Chocolate Crumble (see page 11) made with ¼ tsp (1 mL) freshly grated nutmeg added with the flour

1½ cups (200 g) all-purpose flour

½ cup (55 g) cocoa

1 tsp (5 mL) baking soda

½ tsp (2 mL) baking powder

¼ tsp (1 mL) freshly ground nutmeg

½ tsp (2 mL) kosher salt

½ cup (115 g) butter, slightly softened

1 cup (200 g) sugar

¼ cup (55 g) brown sugar

2 eggs at room temperature

1 cup (250 mL) sour cream

1 tsp (5 mL) vanilla

icing sugar for dusting (optional)

ganache (see page 13) (optional)

1. Preheat the oven to 350°F (180°C). Line a 9-inch (23 cm) square pan or an 8-inch (20 cm) round tube pan with parchment paper, greasing sides and bottom with vegetable spray.

2. Make the Chocolate Crumble and set aside.

3. Mix all the dry ingredients in a bowl and set aside.

4. In the bowl of an electric mixer, beat the butter until soft, scraping the sides and bottom occasionally.

5. Add both sugars and beat on medium speed until light and fluffy, about 10 minutes, scraping the bowl often.

6. Add the eggs 1 at a time, scraping the bowl after each addition and beating until fully incorporated.

7. Mix the sour cream with the vanilla.

8. Alternately add the dry ingredients with the sour cream. Mix on low and turn off the mixer before the last of the flour is fully incorporated.

9. Use a rubber spatula to finish the mixing, gently folding in whatever flour remains visible.

10. Pour and spread the batter evenly in the prepared pan.

11. Sprinkle the crumble evenly over the top.

continued on next page . . .

Chocolate Espresso Coffee Cake (continued)

13. Remove from the oven and let sit in the pan to firm up for about 30 minutes.

14. Unmold and serve with Mocha Ganache (or serve as is dusted with icing sugar).

Mocha Ganache
YIELD: SCANT 2 CUPS (500 ML)

8 oz (227 g) bittersweet chocclate, chopped

1 cup (250 mL) whipping cream

2 Tbsp (30 mL) freshly ground espresso powder

1. Place the chocolate in a medium-sized bowl.

2. Heat the cream in a small saucepan over medium heat.

3. When you see bubbles around the edges, stir in the espresso powder.

4. Just before the cream comes to a boil, remove it from the heat and let it steep for 30 minutes.

5. Return the pan to the heat and bring it to just below a boil.

6. Pour it over the chocolate and let sit for 5 minutes.

7. Whisk it gently until completely smooth.

8. Let it thicken, stirring occasionally to get it to the point where it will wend its way down and around the cake and cling to the sides in thick dribbles, rather than in thin, skimpy streaks. Have patience. The consistency should be that of paint: thick but creamy and still flowing, about 80–85°F (27–30°C).

9. Pour over the cake and let gravity do the work!

BROWNIE POINTER

To make this into a layer cake, grease two 9-inch (23 cm) cake pans with vegetable spray. Preheat the oven to 350°F (180°C). Make the batter and divide between the pans. Bake until a toothpick comes out clean. Cool the layers completely. Meanwhile, make a double batch of the ganache recipe and let it thicken about an hour or so in the fridge, until it has the consistency of sour cream. Slice each cake layer in half horizontally so that you have 4 layers and spread each layer with one-fifth of the ganache, reserving what's left for the sides and top. Press the top of the cake gently. Spread any frosting that has oozed out the sides around the edges to seal any crumbs. Chill for 15 minutes. Remove from the fridge and frost the top and sides with the remaining ganache.

BROWNIE ANGEL FOOD CAKE

YIELD: 8–10 SERVINGS

As a child, I always asked for an angel food cake with vanilla ice cream, fudge sauce and fresh strawberries for my birthday. Looking back, I can't fathom why I'd want such a bland cake. Determined to "brownie it up," I thought long and hard about the logistics of making a moist angel food cake with rich chocolate flavor; I didn't want the egg whites to collapse, but I wanted to make sure I got enough chocolate flavor. Here's the result: I used the recipe for Angel Food Cake by Flo Braker in The Baker's Dozen Cookbook, *and added a little brownie magic. I hope Flo will forgive me for tinkering with her wonderful recipe.*

1¼ cups (315 mL) Classic Brownie batter (see page 29) at room temperature

1½ cups (180 g) icing sugar

1 cup (130 g) cake flour

1½ cups (375 mL) egg whites at room temperature

½ tsp (2 mL) kosher salt

1½ tsp (7 mL) cream of tartar

1 cup (200 g) sugar

icing sugar for dusting

cocoa for dusting

2 pints (300 g) fresh strawberries, sliced

1 Tbsp (15 mL) sugar

1 Tbsp (15 mL) lemon juice

1 cup (250 mL) Chocolate Fudge Sauce (see page 19)

1. Preheat the oven to 350°F (180°C). Have ready an ungreased 10-inch (4 L) tube pan with removable bottom.

2. If you have just made your brownie batter, it will be fluid. If you have refrigerated it, warm it in the microwave on defrost for about 3 minutes or until it is pourable. Stir to make sure it is fluid. Set aside.

3. Sift the icing sugar and cake flour together 3 times. Set aside.

4. Place the egg whites and salt in the bowl of an electric mixer fitted with the whisk attachment, and beat on medium speed until you see a layer of small bubbles. Add the cream of tartar.

5. Increase the speed until soft peaks form.

6. Gradually pour in the 1 cup (200 g) sugar and beat only until soft, droopy peaks form.

7. With the mixer on low speed, gradually pour in 1 cup (250 mL) of the brownie batter. Increase the speed to medium for a few seconds only. You don't want to deflate the egg whites more than necessary.

8. Turn off the mixer, remove the bowl and scrape the batter on the whisk into the bowl.

9. Sprinkle one-third of the flour mixture over the top of the chocolate mixture and fold in gently, using a balloon whisk if possible, or a rubber spatula. Work gently but quickly to incorporate the remaining flour.

10. Pour half of the angel food batter into the pan. Jiggle gently to make it settle evenly.

continued on page 98 . . .

LEMON MARBLE STACK CAKE

YIELD: 8–10 SERVINGS

This is one of those cakes in which mixing the components together would ruin each one, but stacking them allows each to shine. The basic lemon cake recipe and cold oven technique come from a cookbook by Edna Lewis and Scott Peacock, The Gift of Southern Cooking. *I have, however, modified it slightly. By itself or enhanced with brownie batter, the cake is one you'll make over and over again. You'll only use half of the lemon cake batter for this presentation. You can bake the remaining batter in another loaf pan for plain lemon cake, or you can halve the recipe. The cakes freeze very well, wrapped in plastic and foil.*

Cake:

1 cup (227 g) cold butter

1⅔ cups (330 g) sugar

¼ tsp (1 mL) kosher salt

5 eggs at room temperature

2¼ cups (290 g) sifted cake flour

1 Tbsp (15 mL) vanilla extract

1 Tbsp (15 mL) lemon juice

1 lemon, grated rind of

1 cup (250 mL) Classic Brownie batter (see page 29), warm

1. Do not preheat the oven! Grease an 8- × 4-inch (1.5 L) loaf pan with vegetable spray. Line the bottom with overhanging parchment paper.

2. Place the butter in the bowl of an electric mixer fitted with the paddle attachment and beat for about 5 minutes or until waxy and shiny.

3. With the mixer on low speed, gradually add the sugar and salt. Scrape the sides and bottom of the bowl often. Increase the speed to medium and beat for about 5 minutes or until light and fluffy. The mixture will turn white.

4. Add the first 3 eggs 1 at a time, beating and scraping the sides after each addition.

5. After the third egg, add 2 Tbsp (30 mL) of the flour so that the batter doesn't separate. If you forget this step, don't worry, it will come back together again when all the flour is added.

6. Add the remaining eggs 1 at a time, as above.

7. Scrape the sides and bottom of the bowl.

8. Remove the bowl and beater from the mixer. Scrape off any dough sticking to the beater.

9. Mix in the remaining flour gently by hand using a rubber spatula. This ensures a more delicate cake.

10. Finally, add the vanilla, lemon juice and lemon rind.

11. Pour the brownie batter into the bottom of the prepared pan and smooth the top.

continued on page 104 . . .

12. Pour half the lemon cake batter on top of the brownie batter and smooth to make it even. Place the remainder of the lemon cake batter in a second loaf pan, or fill greased muffin tins with it, and bake as follows.

13. Place the pan in the cold oven. Turn the oven to 225°F (105°C) and bake for 20 minutes.

14. Increase the temperature to 300°F (150°C) and bake for an additional 20 minutes.

15. Finally, set the temperature to 325°F (160°C) and bake for 20–30 minutes (for a total baking time of 60–70 minutes) or until a toothpick comes out clean.

16. Remove from the oven and cool on a rack. Run a knife around the edges after 5 or 10 minutes and unmold the cake onto the rack.

17. Make the glaze while the cake cools, and brush it on while the cake is still warm.

Glaze:

⅓ cup (80 mL) freshly squeezed lemon juice

½ cup (100 g) sugar

1 Tbsp (15 mL) butter

⅛ tsp (0.5 mL) kosher salt

1. Place all the ingredients in a small nonreactive saucepan. Stir over medium heat until the sugar is just dissolved.

2. Brush the glaze over the top and sides of the warm cake.

> **BROWNIE POINTER**
>
> To vary this presentation, use both batters to make a marble cake. Pour two-thirds of the lemon cake batter into the pan. Top with the brownie batter. Complete with the remaining lemon batter. Insert a thin knife three-quarters of the way down into the batter and zig-zag around the pan. You won't see the marbling effect until the cake is fully baked and sliced.

Fudgy Pomegranate Pound Cake

YIELD: 10–12 SERVINGS

Every year my parents go down to Florida, and every year, on the eve of their departure, I make a rib roast and create a new dessert. One year, big, plump pomegranates were in season, and it occurred to me that the tartness of the fruit would be a nice counterpoint to chocolate. I was right. Pomegranate molasses is used in the batter and a beautiful pomegranate ganache is used to finish off the cake. The candied walnuts add a pleasant bitterness and crunch, which make this an over-the-top cake. Unlike normal pound cakes, however, this one is nice and moist in the center. You might think it's underdone, but that's the way it's supposed to be! Served warm, it's amazing; served cold or at room temperature, it's terrific.

1¾ cups (225 g) cake flour

1 cup + 2 Tbsp (225 g) sugar

1 tsp (5 mL) baking powder

½ tsp (2 mL) kosher salt

4 eggs at room temperature, lightly beaten

1 Tbsp (15 mL) pomegranate molasses

2 tsp (4 mL) vanilla extract

1 cup (227 g) butter at room temperature

6¼ oz (175 g) bittersweet chocolate, melted (see page vii for tips)

1 cup (250 mL) Candied Walnuts (recipe follows)

1 recipe Pomegranate Icing Sugar Glaze (recipe follows)

1 recipe Pomegranate Ganache (recipe follows)

1. Preheat the oven to 350°F (180°C). Grease an 8- × 4-inch (20 × 10 cm) loaf pan with vegetable spray and line with 1 sheet of overhanging parchment paper.

2. Sift together the flour, sugar, baking powder and salt.

3. Mix together in a separate bowl the eggs, pomegranate molasses and vanilla.

4. In a third bowl beat the butter until softened.

5. Pour the sifted flour mixture into the beaten butter, and add about half of the beaten eggs.

6. Mix on medium speed to moisten. The batter will be thick. Scrape the sides and bottom of the bowl and beat briefly again.

7. Add the remaining eggs and beat on high speed for an additional minute.

8. Remove the bowl from the mixer and scrape the beater.

9. Pour in the cooled, melted chocolate and fold in by hand using a rubber spatula.

10. Scrape the batter into the prepared pan and bake for 30 minutes. Open the oven, and using a serrated knife, make a shallow slit down the center of the cake almost but not completely to each end. This will enable the cake to dome evenly.

11. Set the oven temperature to 325°F (160°C). Bake for an additional 30–35 minutes or until the top is puffed and cracked (but not burned) and a toothpick comes out clean. If at any time the cake looks like it's beginning to brown too much, cover it with aluminum foil until it is done.

continues on next page …

12. While the cake is baking, make the candied walnuts and glazes. Keep the glazes slightly warm.

13. Remove the cake from the oven and let cool for 10 minutes. Unmold onto a cooling rack placed over a plate.

14. Brush the top and sides with the icing sugar glaze. Let set about an hour.

15. Pour the warm ganache over the entire cake and let set, about 30 minutes. It will be shiny.

16. Serve with candied walnuts, pomegranate seeds and crème fraîche.

Candied Walnuts:
YIELD: ABOUT 2 CUPS (250 G)

1 cup (200 g) sugar

3 Tbsp (45 mL) water

1 Tbsp (15 mL) corn syrup

8½ oz (240 g) walnuts, whole or in pieces or both

kosher salt for sprinking

1. Line a baking sheet with parchment paper.

2. In a deep, heavy-bottomed pot, mix all the ingredients together with a rubber spatula.

3. Bring to a boil over high heat. Do not stir from this point on.

4. The sugar will begin to caramelize in about 8 minutes. Watch it carefully to make sure it doesn't burn. When you see the edges getting darker, swirl the pan once or twice.

5. When you begin to smell the caramel, turn the heat down a bit and monitor it until the sugar becomes medium brown in color.

6. Add the walnuts and stir to coat completely.

7. Pour onto the prepared sheet and separate into a single layer using a rubber spatula.

8. Sprinkle a pinch of salt over the top.

9. Let cool. Break into large or small shards.

½ cup (60 g) icing sugar

¼ cup (60 mL) pomegranate juice

teeny pinch kosher salt

2¼ oz (60 g) bittersweet chocolate chips

¼ cup (60 mL) pomegranate juice

1 tsp (5 mL) butter

Pomegranate Icing Sugar Glaze:

1. Place all the ingredients in a small saucepan and bring to a boil.

2. Boil 1 minute and remove from the heat. It should be slightly thickened and smooth. Keep warm.

Pomegranate Ganache:

1. Mix all the ingredients together in a microwaveable bowl.

2. Microwave 2 minutes on high power. Remove and stir until smooth.

BROWNIE POINTER

Pomegranate everything is big news these days because it's thought to have healing properties, not only as an antioxidant but for erectile dysfunction as well (and you thought only brownies cured that!). In fact, pomegranates have been a part of Middle Eastern cuisine for millenia. Pomegranate molasses is nothing more than cooked-down pomegranate juice. It is thick and syrupy, sweet and tart, all at the same time. You will find it at Middle Eastern grocery stores, but now even high-end grocery stores stock it. If you can't find it, though, you can cook down pomegranate juice until it's thick—but you will probably need about 4 times as much juice to get the amount of pomegranate molasses. (Note that regular molasses is not a substitute.)

Coffee Orange Pound Cake with Cocoa Nibs

YIELD: 10 SLICES

How did this emphatically nonchocolate cake get into this book? Because it is as good as any chocolate cake, the mix of coffee, orange and cocoa nibs totally irresistible. It will become a staple in your kitchen. It's great toasted, too, or just all by itself.

½ cup (65 g) all-purpose flour

¼ cup (30 g) cocoa

½ tsp (2 mL) baking powder

¼ tsp (1 mL) kosher salt

7 oz (200 g) almond paste

1 cup (200 g) sugar

1 orange, grated rind of

1 cup (227 g) butter at room temperature

5 eggs

2 Tbsp (30 mL) strong coffee or espresso

1 tsp (5 mL) vanilla extract

¼ cup (30 g) cocoa nibs (see Brownie Pointer on page 45)

1 recipe Coffee Grand Marnier Glaze (recipe follows)

1 oz (28 g) sliced almonds, toasted

1. Preheat the oven to 350°F (180°C). Line an 8- × 4-inch (20 × 10 cm) loaf pan with parchment paper and grease the sides with vegetable spray.

2. Sift together the flour, cocoa, baking powder and salt.

3. Place the almond paste in the bowl of an electric mixer fitted with the paddle attachment or in the bowl of a food processor with the metal blade. Beat/process until smooth.

4. With the machine on, gradually add the sugar and orange rind. Mix until the sugar and almond paste are well blended.

5. Cut the butter into pieces and add gradually, beating or pulsing (depending upon which type of machine you are using) until the mixture is uniform. (Don't overpulse in the food processor since it will melt the butter.)

6. Add the eggs 1 at a time, beating well after each addition.

7. Add the coffee and vanilla and mix until blended.

8. Add the flour mixture all at once and mix on low speed only until a bit of flour is still visible. You don't want to overmix it.

9. Remove the bowl from the mixer or food processor. Add the cocoa nibs and fold in until the streaks of flour are no longer visible.

10. Pour the batter into the prepared pan and place in the oven.

11. Set the timer to 20 minutes. When the timer goes off, a crust should have appeared on the top of the cake. With a serrated knife, make a shallow slash down the center of the cake from about ½ inch (1 cm) in from either end. It will be liquidy beneath the crust, but that's okay. This slash will enable the cake to mound nicely in the center.

12. Bake for another 30–40 minutes (total baking time: 50–60 minutes) or until a toothpick inserted in the brownies comes out clean.

13. While the cake is baking making the Coffee Grand Marnier Glaze.

14. Don't remove the cake from the pan immediately. It is a delicate cake so it needs to sit for about 15 minutes in the pan, but do not let it cool completely.

continued on page 110 . . .

Dominique and
Cindy Duby

15. When ready to remove, run a knife around the edges and lift it out using the parchment paper "handles."

16. Brush the glaze all over the sides and top.

17. In a small bowl, drizzle a bit of glaze over the almonds just enough to moisten them. Distribute them evenly over the top of the cake.

Coffee Grand Marnier Glaze:

3 Tbsp (45 mL) strong-brewed coffee or espresso

3 Tbsp (45 mL) Grand Marnier

¾ cup (150 g) sugar

pinch kosher salt

1. Mix together all the ingredients in a saucepan.

2. Set over medium heat and bring to a boil. Turn the heat off. All the sugar won't melt. This is good!

BROWNIE POINTERS

• Make sure that the cake is warm or else it won't absorb the glaze as much. I find that sometimes the cake takes all the glaze, and sometimes there's some left over. In the latter case, I wait for the cake to cool and pour the remaining glaze over the top.

• The original, *original* glaze recipe comes from Flo Braker's stupendous book *The Simple Art of Perfect Baking*. Both she and the patissier with whom I trained don't heat the glaze at all. That way, the glaze tends to harden a bit, forming a wonderfully delicate, crisp and shiny coating as opposed to being absorbed by the cake.

Seville Orange Marble Chocolate Cake

YIELD: 8 SERVINGS

Orange-and-chocolate is often a serendipitous combination, but I think they were meant to go together: oranges and cacao both grow on trees in the tropics, and both are acidic, yet their acidity seems to complement rather than compete with each other. This is a marbled tea cake featuring both flavors, in "adult" form, making this cake surprisingly sophisticated—Seville oranges and bitter dark chocolate. It's the Seville that makes Seville marmalade splendid: sweet and sour at the same time, with a tinge of bitterness that offsets the sugar, resulting in an irresistible combination. Make the marmalade from scratch and you will have enough left over to slather either on a toasted slice of this cake or your breakfast toast.

4 oz (113 g) unsweetened chocolate, coarsely chopped

2 Tbsp (30 mL) sugar

1½ cups (200 g) all-purpose flour

½ cup (65 g) whole wheat flour

1½ tsp (10 mL) baking powder

½ tsp (2 mL) kosher salt

¼ tsp (1 mL) freshly ground nutmeg

¾ cup (170 g) butter at room temperature

1 cup (200 g) sugar

scant ¾ cup (190 mL) Seville Orange Marmalade, plus 1 Tbsp (15 mL) for the glaze (see page 38)

4 eggs

1 Tbsp (15 mL) Grand Marnier or orange juice

2 Tbsp (30 mL) ganache (see page 13) (optional)

1. Preheat the oven to 350°F (180°C). Lightly grease and line an 8- × 4-inch (20 × 10 cm) loaf pan with parchment paper.

2. Melt the chopped chocolate in a bowl set in a pan of simmering water. When it's almost completely melted, remove from the heat and let the residual heat melt the remaining chocolate. Add the 2 Tbsp (30 mL) sugar and stir to blend. Set aside.

3. Mix together the flours, baking powder, salt and nutmeg.

4. Beat the butter and sugar in a mixer until light and fluffy. Add the marmalade and beat just until incorporated.

5. Add the eggs, 1 at a time, scraping the sides and bottom after adding each one.

6. Add the flour mixture, and mix only until blended. In fact, stop the mixer when there is still flour to be blended and finish by hand. The batter will be thick.

7. Remove half the batter into another bowl. Fold in the melted chocolate.

8. Spread the chocolate batter into the prepared pan, then top with the other half of the batter. After 30 minutes in the oven, use a knife to make a slit down the center of the cake to allow it to dome as much as possible.

9. After about 45 minutes, if the crust is darkening too much, place a piece of aluminum foil over the cake and reduce the heat to 325°F (160°C).

10. When your kitchen smells amazing, and a toothpick inserted into the center comes out clean—about 60 minutes—remove the cake from the oven. You will hear slow bubbles crackling if you put the cake to your ear.

continued on next page...

11. In a small saucepan, stir together 1 Tbsp (15 mL) of the marmalade and add 1 Tbsp (15 mL) of the Grand Marnier. Place on the heat and bring to a boil.

12. Poke the cake all over with a toothpick and brush the nubby glaze over the top.

13. Drizzle with the optional ganache, or serve as is.

BROWNIE POINTER

If you also have a loved one like my husband Howard who isn't too fond of sweets that are sour, an alternative would be to squeeze the juice and grate the rind when you make the marmalade, leaving out the extra-bitter pith. This will result in a cake with noticeably less bite. You could also substitute the unsweetened chocolate with a semisweet chocolate that has a cocoa content of between 60% and 65%.

Flourless Chocolate Cake

This was formerly known as Fallen Soufflé Cake because it would rise in the oven and collapse when cool, leaving a higher edge and a cracked crust frequently hidden under a light sprinkling of icing sugar. It wasn't bad. It just didn't reach its potential until I stumbled on a new technique. If you make and bake this the same day, the cake will rise and then settle somewhat, but if you prepare the batter the day before, chill it in the fridge overnight, and then bake it, the result will be, for some reason I can't figure out, a cake that doesn't settle as much, with a light, custardy, but definitely fudgy consistency. If possible, eat it while still warm. It's incredible.

1 lb (454 g) bittersweet chocolate, chopped

1 cup (227 g) cold butter, cubed

½ cup (100 g) sugar

6 eggs

1 Tbsp (15 mL) Kahlúa or brewed coffee

½ tsp (2 mL) kosher salt

2 cups (500 mL) whipped cream

1. Place a 10-inch (25 cm) square piece of parchment paper over the bottom of a 9-inch (23 cm) springform pan. Fit the exterior ring over the base and close. This should create a waterproof barrier. If you are in doubt, wrap the bottom of the pan in foil that goes three-quarters of the way up the outside. Grease the pan with vegetable spray.

2. Melt the chocolate and butter in a saucepan over low heat.

3. When the chocolate, but not all of the butter, is melted, remove the bowl from the heat and allow the heat of the chocolate to melt the remaining butter. Stir to blend well. Let cool a bit. Set aside.

4. Place the sugar and eggs in the bowl of an electric mixer and fit with the whisk attachment. Beat on high speed for about 5 minutes or until light and triple in volume.

5. Turn the mixer to the lowest speed and pour in the chocolate mixture. Continue to mix until the chocolate is completely incorporated.

6. Add the Kahlúa and salt.

7. Pour the batter into the prepared pan. At this point, you can either bake the cake following the instructions in step 10 or cover the pan tightly with plastic wrap and refrigerate for 8 hours or overnight.

8. When you are ready to bake the cake, preheat the oven to 300°F (150°C). Boil about 4 cups (1 L) of water.

9. Place the cake batter in the prepared cake pan, then place this pan in a roasting pan in the oven. Fill the roasting pan with enough boiling water to reach three-quarters up the sides of the cake pan.

continued on next page...

The Buns:

1. Preheat the oven to 350°F (180°C). For the best-looking finish, line a 9- × 13-inch (23 × 33 cm) brownie pan with overhanging parchment paper.

2. Spread the pan schmear evenly on the pan bottom. Sprinkle the pecans in an even layer on top. Set aside while you roll the dough.

3. Sprinkle your work surface lightly with flour. Place the chocolate challah dough on the counter and press it gently into a rough rectangle.

4. Roll the dough to a thickness of about ¼ inch (5 mm). Keep lifting and flipping it over, sprinkling the rolling surface lightly with flour. If the dough resists rolling and springs back, let it rest, covered loosely with a kitchen towel, for 5–10 minutes.

5. Roll the dough into a rectangle about 8 × 16 inches (20 × 40 cm) (with the long side toward you).

6. Spread the brownie batter evenly over the dough, then brush with the melted butter. Sprinkle 3 Tbsp (45 mL) of the cinnamon, cocoa and sugar mixture over the brownie batter-slathered dough. Sprinkle the chocolate chips and raisins evenly over all.

7. Starting at the side nearest you, place your thumbs under the bottom edge, and begin rolling toward the top. Every time you are about to roll up, gently pull the dough down towards you and give it a slight tug to stretch it towards you. This will extend the dough and make a tighter roll. Roll it up completely. Pinch the seam closed. Place it seam side down on the counter.

8. Place both hands over the center of the dough and gently squeeze and roll as you move your hands out to the sides. This will even out the roll, which tends to be fat in the center and thin at the ends. Don't worry if this happens. You won't notice it in the final product.

9. Use a ruler to make notches 1 inch (2.5 cm) apart. Cut the roll into 12–16 slices. Place each slice cut side up in the prepared pan. Don't worry if it's not symmetrical. When the dough rises, the rolls will touch each other and fill in the spaces. They will come out of the pan looking great.

continued on next page . . .

BROWNIE POINTER

Some might think this suggestion is overdoing it, but a yummy addition to the buns is to make a simple icing sugar glaze by whisking ½ cup (60 g) icing sugar with 2 Tbsp (30 mL) milk or cream and adding some freshly grated orange rind or ¼ tsp (1 mL) of almond extract. Drizzle this all over the cinnamon buns.

10. Cover the pan with plastic wrap. At this point, you can put the buns in the fridge overnight. Allow them to sit at room temperature for at least an hour before baking the next day.

11. If you want to bake them the same day, place the covered pan in a warm place and allow to rise. This will take about 1½ hours, depending upon how warm the room is. The buns are ready to be baked when the dough keeps an indentation when gently pressed with your finger and is at least as high as the edge of the pan, if not higher by ½ inch (1 cm).

12. Preheat the oven to 350°F (180°C).

13. Place the pan in the oven and bake for 25–35 minutes. Because this is a chocolate dough, it is difficult to determine when the buns are ready. They don't "brown" like white bread dough. Trust your instincts: if you smell something wonderful, they are close to being ready. Poke the dough with your finger. If it is firm, it is ready. The centers will be softer than the edges but resist the temptation to overbake . . . there's nothing like warm, soft centers oozing chocolate!

14. Let the buns sit for 5 minutes before turning them upside down onto a serving platter. Turning them out of the pan while they are still warm makes sure that they come out in 1 piece and that all the schmear, now baked into amazing goo, follows. If there's any goo remaining in the pan, use a spatula to lift it out while it's still liquid and spread it on top of the buns.

15. These are best eaten the day they are made. But in the unlikely event that any are left over, cover with plastic wrap and reheat gently before serving the next day.

16. The unbaked, prepared buns may be frozen in the pan for future use. Cover tightly with plastic wrap and foil. Make sure the dough is completely defrosted and has risen before placing it in the oven to bake.

Crunchy, Munchy Brownie Cookies

Ultimate, Ultimate Chocolate Chunk Cookies

YIELD: 18 BIG COOKIES

Everyone calls their chocolate chunk cookies "the ultimate," but mine are the real deal. How do I know? I brought these into work one day to get a reaction from some of the most critical, best-informed food people I know and they all raved about them! Once you make them, you won't turn back to those imposters! Oat flour is found in natural food stores or in the natural food section of many supermarkets. If you can't find it, pulse rolled oats to a fine powder in the food processor.

2 oz (56 g) walnuts, coarsely chopped

2 oz (56 g) pecans, coarsely chopped

½ cup (50 g) coconut

½ cup (45 g) rolled oats (not quick cooking)

1 cup (130 g) all-purpose flour

½ cup (65 g) oat flour

¾ tsp (3 mL) baking soda

½ tsp (2 mL) kosher salt

¼ tsp (1 mL) ground cinnamon

¾ cup (170 g) butter

¾ cup (165 g) brown sugar

¾ cup *less* 1 Tbsp (140 g) granulated sugar

2 eggs

1 tsp (5 mL) vanilla extract

12 oz (340 g) milk chocolate, chopped into chip-sized pieces

12 oz (340 g) bittersweet chocolate, chopped into chip-sized pieces

1. Preheat the oven to 350°F (180°C).

2. Place the walnuts and pecans on a cookie sheet and toast for 12 minutes.

3. Place the coconut and rolled oats on a separate cookie sheet and toast for about 10 minutes, tossing occasionally until just golden brown. Don't overbake. Set the nuts and coconut mixture aside.

4. Mix the flour, oat flour, baking soda, baking powder, salt and cinnamon in a medium bowl.

5. In the bowl of an electric mixer beat the butter until soft, about 2 minutes.

6. Add both sugars and blend for an additional 2 minutes, scraping the sides and bottom of the bowl once or twice.

7. Add the eggs 1 at a time, scraping the bowl between additions.

8. Add the vanilla and mix briefly.

9. Add the dry ingredients and mix just until barely blended.

10. Add the nuts and coconut mixture. Mix for about 1 minute.

11. Remove the bowl from the mixer and add both chocolates, folding them into the batter with a rubber spatula.

12. Use a 3 oz (85 g) scoop to portion the cookies 3 inches (8 cm) apart on a cookie sheet.

13. Bake for 10–12 minutes, or until the cookies are golden and firm around the edges but still a bit soft in the center.

14. Let them cool slightly before removing from the baking sheet onto a cooling rack.

CLOCKWISE FROM LEFT ▶
Brownie Blobs (page 126), Ultimate, Ultimate Chocolate
Chunk Cookies (this page), Chocolate Rugelah (page 140)
Deconstructed Chocolate Halvah Cookies (page 136)

Spiced Chocolate Biscotti (continued)

BROWNIE POINTER

Do I really have to tell you that if you dip these in melted dark or white chocolate they will be that much more delicious?!

15. Sprinkle the tops with the remaining cinnamon sugar.

16. Bake in the oven an additional 15–20 minutes or until they feel crisp to the touch. Transfer the biscotti to a wire rack. They will crisp up further as they cool.

17. Store in a tightly sealed container for, oh, at least a month or more.

Mom's Crunch Center Cookies (continued)

1 recipe Pecan Praline, chopped

6 oz (170 g) milk chocolate, coarsely
   chopped

1 cup (120 g) icing sugar, sifted

6. Add the chopped praline. Some of it will not incorporate but will stay on the bottom of the bowl.

7. Add the chopped chocolate and mix briefly.

8. Remove the bowl from the mixer and, using your hands, lightly knead the dough to mix in any chunks of chocolate and praline that have resisted incorporation.

9. Place walnut-sized balls of dough on a cookie sheet using your hands to lightly roll them into rough rounds.

10. Bake for 10 minutes and remove from the oven. At this point, cookies are too fragile to remove from the pan.

11. Cool for about 10–15 minutes until they are firm enough to remove using a metal spatula. Some of them will have tails of pooled, crisp praline attached to them. This is good!

12. Place the sifted icing sugar in a bowl. Gently roll each slightly warm cookie in the icing sugar. Some of it will melt. This is okay. Served warm or at room temperature, these cookies are irresistible.

BIG, FAT BIG-APPLE COOKIES
(AKA ABBY'S FAVORITE COOKIES)

YIELD: ABOUT 12 COOKIES

My sister Abby is fond of finding cookies wherever she travels and returning with a tiny morsel for me so I can, as she puts it, "reverse engineer" the cookie—that is, copy it. These big, fat chocolate cookies are based on a cookie she brought from a teeny-tiny basement bakery in New York City. The two of us rarely have time to cook together these days, but when we do, as we did for our dad's 84th birthday, there is much laughter, bonding and sharing, which is what a lot of women did back in the "old days" when they were expected to be in the kitchen most of the time. Our liberated selves find the kitchen a comforting retreat from the hurly-burly of our busy lives. And these cookies are, well, amazing. Big and fat and loaded with chocolate, they are not for the fainthearted and are great to share with your sister . . . even if it's not in the kitchen.

scant 1½ cup (180 g) whole wheat flour

generous ⅔ cup (80 g) cocoa

1¾ tsp (8 mL) baking powder

½ tsp (2 mL) kosher salt

½ cup + 2 Tbsp (140 g) butter

½ cup (100 g) sugar

2 tsp (10 mL) vanilla extract

1 egg

6 oz (170 g) bittersweet chocolate, chopped in chunks

1½–2 cups (150–200 g) toasted walnut pieces

1. Preheat the oven to 350°F (180°C). Grease or line a cookie sheet with parchment paper.

2. In a bowl, mix the flour, cocoa, baking powder and salt. Set aside.

3. Place the butter in a mixing bowl and beat on low speed until softened. Add the sugar and beat until smooth but not fluffy.

4. Add the vanilla and beat just until smooth.

5. Add the egg and beat until smooth.

6. Add the dry ingredients. Mix until just until blended.

7. Add the chocolate chunks and the walnuts. Mix until incorporated. Some of the chocolate and nuts may still sit on the bottom of the bowl: Remove the bowl from the mixer, and with a wooden spoon or your hands carefully press the dough (which will be stiff) into a ball, picking up the pieces of nuts and chocolate on the bottom. Rotate the dough, picking up what remains in the bottom of the bowl.

8. Make sure the dough is slightly stiff, definitely not soft, before scooping. If the dough softens, place it in the fridge for 20 minutes.

9. Drop blobs, about 2–3 large tablespoons in size, onto the cookie sheet. About 6 or 8 should fit per sheet.

10. Press flat with the palm of your hand.

11. Bake for 10–12 minutes depending upon the size. The bigger the blob the longer the baking time should be, but make sure that you don't overbake them. They will puff but still be soft to the touch when done. They will firm up when cool.

12. Transfer the cookies to a wire rack and cool. Store in a sealed container.

BROWNIE POINTERS

- Reduce the amount of chocolate chunks by half and substitute with some good quality, large juicy raisins (not the tiny and overly sweet kids' raisins).

- This is a perfect cookie to spice up a bit with some cayenne pepper! This would make it similar to the chocolate the Mayan Indians, the true chocolate innovators, used to consume. Add about ¼–½ tsp (2–5 mL) cayenne pepper to the flour and mix as above.

PEASANT MACAROONS

YIELD: ABOUT 20 TABLESPOON-SIZED COOKIES

Why "Peasant" Macaroons? Because they have all the ingredients of French macaroons without the fuss: no nut flour, no piping but incredible flavor and crunch, with a rustic, handmade look.

5½ oz (155 g) toasted almonds

2 oz (56 g) toasted walnuts

1½ oz (45 g) toasted hazelnuts

1 cup (200 g) sugar

3 Tbsp (20 g) cocoa

¼ tsp (1 mL) cinnamon

¼ tsp (1 mL) instant espresso powder

pinch kosher salt

2 egg whites

1. Preheat the oven to 350°F (180°C). Line 2 cookie sheets with parchment paper.

2. Place a large saucepan filled one-quarter of the way with water over medium heat. Bring to a simmer.

3. Place all the nuts, sugar, cocoa, cinnamon, espresso powder and pinch salt in the bowl of a food processor fitted with a steel blade.

4. Pulse on and off until the nuts are coarsely ground. It's okay if there are finely ground nuts in with the larger pieces. Chopping by hand takes more time but you will get a more uniform nut. Either way, the cookie works, so don't sweat the decision: Food processor? Knife? Just don't process everything to nut butter!

5. Pour the nut mixture into a bowl along with the egg whites and set it over the pot of simmering water, stirring constantly with a rubber spatula.

6. When the whites begin to melt the sugar and the mixture becomes warm to the touch remove it from the heat.

7. Drop teaspoonsful of batter onto the prepared pans, leaving about 2 inches (5 cm) between cookies.

8. Bake 20 minutes, and then cool on the cookie sheets.

9. When completely cooled, the cookies will be amazingly crisp and addictive.

10. Store in a tight container, away from any humidity, for about a week.

SERIOUSLY DELICIOUS
CHOCOLATE ORANGE GINGERSNAPS

YIELD: ABOUT FIFTY-FIVE 1 OZ (28 G) COOKIES

Proust had his madeleines, I have my gingersnaps. My mother's were chewy rounds with a crunchy sugary coating. Made exclusively with ground ginger, they had—for the '60s—more zing than most baked goods. Fast forward 30 years: San Francisco airport in the early '80s. At the Starbucks (a harbinger of the future for sure!) was a chewy gingerbread cookie four inches in diameter, thicker than Mom's but just as delicious. And finally, I recently found myself in Ann Arbor's famous Zingerman's Bakehouse where looking straight at me was a dark disc studded with big bits of Demerara sugar. It was different from the other two, but perfectly suited to my adult taste buds as it was loaded with three kinds of ginger: fresh, dried and candied. I set out to duplicate it but with chocolate. I had come upon a gingersnap recipe in Heirloom Baking with the Brass Sisters, *which called for marmalade. Well, I had two jars of homemade Seville orange marmalade (a variety more astringent than normal—see page 38 for a recipe), and I knew that orange and ginger are wonderful with chocolate—and so this recipe was born.*

1 cup + 2 Tbsp (145 g) all-purpose flour	1. Line cookie sheets with parchment paper.
¼ cup + 2 Tbsp (40 g) cocoa	2. Mix the dry ingredients together using a whisk.
2 tsp (10 mL) baking soda	3. In a mixer, beat together the butter and sugars on low speed until well blended. Stop and scrape the bottom and sides as required.
2 tsp (10 mL) ground ginger	
1 tsp (5 mL) cinnamon	4. Add the molasses, marmalade and grated ginger, and mix to blend.
1 tsp (5 mL) freshly grated nutmeg	5. Add the egg and vanilla and mix. Batter may look curdled, but that's okay. Stop and scrap the sides and bottom of the mixing bowl.
½ tsp (2 mL) kosher salt	
¾ cup (170 g) cold butter, in pieces	6. Add the dry ingredients all at once, and on low speed mix until it's just incorporated. By this time the batter will be thick.
¾ cup (150 g) granulated sugar	
½ cup (110 g) brown sugar	7. Add the candied ginger, cocoa nibs, and chopped chocolate. Mix only until incorporated.
¼ cup (60 mL) molasses	
¼ cup (60 mL) bitter orange marmalade, preferably Seville (see page 38)	8. Spread the batter in a 9- × 13-inch (23 × 33 cm) baking pan so the batter will cool quickly and evenly. Refrigerate for 30 minutes.
	9. Fifteen minutes prior to baking, preheat your oven to 350°F (180°C).
	10. Pour the Demerara sugar onto a plate.

continued on page 147…

Seriously Delicious Chocolate Orange Gingersnaps (continued)

1 heaping Tbsp (20 mL) peeled and grated fresh ginger

1 egg

1 tsp (5 mL) vanilla extract

5 Tbsp (50 g) finely chopped candied ginger

2 Tbsp (30 mL) cocoa nibs (see Brownie Pointer on page 45)

5 Tbsp (50 g) 70% (or higher) bittersweet chocolate, chopped to the size of rice grains

2 cups (400 g) Demerara sugar

11. Using a small scoop or a teaspoon, portion a blob of batter, and with your hands roll it into a ball.

12. Drop the ball into the sugar and roll to coat completely.

13. Place a maximum of 10 balls on each cookie sheet. Refer to the Brownie Pointers in order to decide whether or not you need to flatten and/or refrigerate the balls, and how long to bake them. Left alone in a cookie jar, they will stay fresh for about a week or more.

> ## BROWNIE POINTERS
>
> Do you like your cookies chewy or crisp? How they end up depends on three factors: how cold they are when they go into the oven; whether they are ball-shaped or flattened before baking; and how long they are baked.
>
> - For entirely crisp cookies, flatten the balls slightly with the palm of your hand and bake for about 5–6 minutes or until you see cracks on top and they have collapsed. They will puff and then flatten as they bake. Cool completely on the baking sheets.
>
> - For cookies that are crisp around the edges but chewy in the center, chill the shaped cookies for about 10 minutes prior to baking. Don't flatten the cookies. Pull out of the oven just when they puff up the most—about 10–11 minutes—and let cool completely in the pan.
>
> - For thicker cookies, see the recipe for Brownie Molasses Ginger Cookies (page 148), which is as close as I can get to Zingerman's amazing cookie.
>
> - These cookies can also be frozen. Roll the dough into balls, coat them with sugar and freeze them. They are ready to be baked straight from the freezer, only adjust the baking time to a bit longer. You can also freeze already-baked cookies: wrap them tightly, and you can nibble on frozen (or thawed) cookies anytime.

FUDGY BROWNIE CHRISTMAS PUDDING

YIELD: 10–12 SERVINGS

I buy a lot of esoteric baking equipment on the assumption that one day I'll use it . . . which is how I came to own a classic Christmas pudding mold, a kind of deep Bundt pan with a snap-on lid. The pan sat in the basement for about 10 years until I was asked to do demos for a steam oven. The pan's time had come!

one 8 oz (250 mL) jar Lyle's Golden Syrup

½ cup (55 g) cocoa

½ cup (125 mL) hot water

2 Tbsp (30 mL) instant coffee granules

1 cup (227 g) butter at room temperature

1 cup + 2 Tbsp (250 g) brown sugar

6 eggs

1 cup (130 g) all-purpose flour

½ tsp (2 mL) baking soda

5 oz (140 g) bittersweet chocolate, chopped

BROWNIE POINTER

Alternatively, you can place the pudding pan on top of an empty tuna can set in a large, wide pot, such as a canning or soup pot. Add enough boiling water to come halfway up the sides of the pudding pan and seal with the lid. Cook on the stove over heat low enough to keep the water at a gentle simmer for about 1½ hours. Replenish the water if it becomes too low.

1. Preheat the oven to 350°F (180°C). Bring a pot of water to a simmer while you prepare the batter. Have ready a roasting pan with 4-inch (10 cm) or higher sides.

2. Grease a traditional pudding pan or 2 qt (2 L) Bundt with vegetable spray.

3. Pour the golden syrup into the bottom of the prepared container.

4. Mix the cocoa, hot water and instant coffee in a small bowl until smooth. Set aside.

5. Place the butter, brown sugar and eggs in the bowl of a food processor. Pulse until smooth.

6. Add the cocoa mixture and pulse again, scraping the sides of the bowl.

7. Add the flour and baking soda and pulse just until blended.

8. Add the chocolate and pulse once or twice.

9. With a rubber spatula, scrape into the prepared pan and seal with the top if you have a steamer pan, or cover tightly with foil.

10. Set the pudding pan in the roasting pan and place in the oven. Pour boiling water half of the way up the sides of the pudding pan.

11. Bake in the oven for about 1–1½ hours or until the pudding is puffed. You can remove the top to check.

12. Remove the pudding pan and remove the top or foil. Place a wide plate over the top and turn upside down. The pudding will plop out surrounded by a nice, gooey sauce.

13. Enjoy while hot and serve with vanilla ice cream, sour cream or crème fraîche.

CRÈME CHOCOMEL

YIELD: 8 SERVINGS

Is it a pudding or a custard? Who cares! It's fabulous and easy. Feel free to substitute your favorite liqueur if you don't like licorice. Raspberry, blackcurrant (crème de cassis), orange, rum, brandy and whisky all work equally well. While you can serve the Crème Chocomel straight out of the oven, the glossy caramelized topping requires that the crème be completely chilled first, so plan accordingly.

1⅓ cups (330 mL) whipping cream

6 oz (170 g) bittersweet chocolate, chopped

2 eggs

2 egg yolks

1 Tbsp (15 mL) licorice liqueur, such as Pernod

½ cup (100 g) sugar for caramelizing

BROWNIE POINTER

Small propane torches are now available at kitchen specialty stores. Keep the flame pointed almost straight over the sugar while waving it back and forth to avoid burning the sugar.

Plan to caramelize the puddings a few minutes before serving them. If you place the chilled, caramelized puddings back into the fridge, the sugar will eventually turn to syrup, losing its crunch completely.

---

1. Preheat the oven to 300°F (150°C). Have ready eight 4 oz (125 mL) ramekins or custard cups, a roasting pan large enough to hold them all with space between, and simmering water.

2. Heat the cream in a small saucepan over low heat.

3. Place the chocolate in a bowl and pour the cream overtop. Allow to cool, whisking occasionally. Set aside.

4. Whisk the eggs, yolks and liqueur together. Add ¼ cup (60 mL) of the chocolate mixture to the eggs. Pour the tempered egg mixture through a strainer into the chocolate mixture and whisk.

5. Pour the chocolate cream into the ramekins filling them three-quarters full. Place the roasting pan in the oven and the ramekins in the roasting pan.

6. Pour enough boiling water into the roasting pan to come halfway up the sides of the ramekins.

7. Bake for about 20–25 minutes or until there is a quarter-sized area in the center of each dish that is still jiggly. Remove from the oven.

8. Remove ramekins from the water bath and let cool completely. Chill thoroughly.

9. Sprinkle each custard with a thin coating of sugar. Using a propane torch or oven broiler, caramelize the top until it is golden brown and crisp. Be careful not to let the sugar catch fire or a burned taste will permeate the pudding.

10. Serve immediately.

CHOCOLATE COCONUT CRÈME CARAMEL

YIELD: 6 SERVINGS

This recipe needs to be made ahead of time and chilled if you want the full impact of the caramel oozing around the unmolded custard. If you don't care, you can eat it warm, but the caramel sticks to the inside of the cup. It's a tropical alternative to that all-time comfort food, crème caramel, and is equally pleasing, but lighter in texture and taste. It's also nondairy.

½ cup (100 g) granulated sugar

2 Tbsp (30 mL) brown sugar

6½ oz (185 g) bittersweet chocolate, chopped

1 can (13.5 oz/400 mL) coconut milk, shaken well

pinch kosher salt

2 eggs

1 egg yolk

¼ cup (25 g) sweetened coconut, toasted

1. Preheat the oven to 300°F (150°C). Have ready 6 ramekins or 4 oz (125 mL) custard cups, a kettle of simmering water and a roasting pan large enough to hold the ramekins with space between.

2. Place both sugars in a small saucepan. Add 3 Tbsp (45 mL) water. Stir briefly.

3. Bring to a boil and cover. Boil for 3 minutes.

4. Remove the cover and let the water evaporate and the sugar caramelize. If the sugar begins to brown in one area of the pan, gently swirl it to redistribute the sugar.

5. When the sugar is a deep golden brown, divide it among the ramekins. Lift each cup and swirl the sugar so it coats the bottom and some of the sides. Set aside to cool.

6. Place the chopped chocolate in a bowl. In a medium saucepan, heat the coconut milk to just below a boil.

7. Pour the coconut milk over the chopped chocolate. Let sit for about 10 minutes. Add the salt.

8. Gently whisk the coconut milk and chocolate together to make a silky smooth blend. Cool for about 10 minutes.

9. Whisk together the eggs and egg yolk. Drizzle into the chocolate mixture, whisking until smooth.

10. Pour into the ramekins, filling them three-quarters full.

11. Place the ramekins in the roasting pan and the roasting pan in the oven. Pour boiling water into the roasting pan halfway up the sides of the pots.

continued on next page . . .

Chocolate Coconut Crème Caramel (continued)

12. Bake for 20–25 minutes or until the edges are firm but there is a quarter-sized area in the center that is still jiggly.

13. Remove from the oven and let the custards cool completely. Chill for a minimum of 3 hours or until completely set.

14. Run the tip of a knife around the edges to release the custards. Place a small plate on top and flip the cup and plate. Gently lift the cup. Sugar syrup will surround the released pudding.

15. Serve sprinkled with the toasted coconut.

Pot de Crème à la Minute

YIELD: 4 OR 8 SERVINGS, DEPENDING ON THE CONTAINER

What, another pudding recipe? After a childhood without pudding and an adulthood in search of the perfect one, I can never have enough. You won't be able to resist either.

½ cup (125 mL) half-and-half cream

1 tsp (5 mL) instant coffee granules

2½ oz (70 g) bittersweet chocolate, chopped

1 egg

1 egg yolk

2 Tbsp (30 mL) sugar

2 tsp (10 mL) Kahlúa or brewed coffee

1 tsp (5 mL) vanilla extract

½ cup (125 mL) whipping cream

1 Tbsp (15 mL) Kahlúa or instant coffee granules

grated bittersweet chocolate or chocolate curls for garnish

1. Preheat the oven to 300°F (150°C). Have ready simmering water, 8 demitasse or four 4 oz (125 mL) custard cups and a roasting pan.

2. Heat the cream and instant coffee in a small saucepan. Bring it to just below boiling.

3. Remove from the heat and add the chocolate. Stir gently to melt. Try not to incorporate any air bubbles. Set aside.

4. Gently whisk together the egg, yolk, sugar, the 2 tsp (10 mL) Kahlúa and vanilla.

5. Pour a little chocolate cream into the egg mixture and whisk gently. Pour the remaining chocolate cream into the egg mix and stir gently to incorporate until silky and smooth. Strain into a 2-cup (500 mL) measure with spout.

6. Pour into the cups, filling them three-quarters full.

7. Place the cups a few inches apart in the roasting pan. Place the pan in the oven and pour boiling water in the outer pan to come halfway up the sides of the cups.

8. Bake for 15–20 minutes or until the custard is firm around the edges but still jiggly in the center. It will continue to cook when you remove the pan from the oven.

9. Remove the cups from the water bath and let cool slightly.

10. While these are best served warm, they may be served at room temperature or chilled and served the next day.

11. Garnish with whipped cream flavored with the 1 Tbsp (15 mL) Kahlúa and grated chocolate or chocolate curls (or more simply with some cold, cold cream poured on top of the hot puddings and dusted with cocoa).

- While you may not have half-and-half (i.e., 10% cream) on hand, you might have vanilla ice cream. I find it is a wonderful substitute when a recipe calls for cream. I have made everything from caramel sauce to pot de crème au chocolat by substituting with vanilla ice cream. Just melt the amount you need and use it as if it were regular cream. You might want to tone down the sugar a bit, but it's not critical.

- This recipe can easily be doubled or quadrupled for more servings. Just make sure the water bath allows plenty of room between the cups.

- Chocolate curls are easy to make if you have a good, sharp vegetable peeler. The warmer the chocolate, the easier it is to get nice curls. You can warm chocolate the way professionals do by stroking the surface with the palm of your hand! Milk chocolate works best but bittersweet will work too. Hold the chocolate in one hand and use the peeler to strip chocolate off 1 of the edges. Let the curls fall onto a piece of parchment paper. Keep in a covered container away from heat.

Chocolate To(fu)s de Crème
(Vegan Pots de Crème)

YIELD: 6 SERVINGS

I developed this dessert for a cooking class where one person was vegan. It turned out so well that most guests didn't realize it was vegan at all!

1 cup (250 mL) soy milk

5½ oz (155 g) bittersweet chocolate, chopped in chunks

½ cup + 1 Tbsp (115 g) sugar

½ cup (125 mL) firm tofu

¼ cup (30 g) cocoa

3 Tbsp (45 mL) coffee

1 Tbsp (15 mL) rum

pinch kosher salt

1. Preheat the oven to 300°F (150°C).

2. Have ready 6 espresso cups, a brownie pan and a pot of boiling water.

3. Heat the soy milk to a gentle simmer.

4. Place the remaining ingredients into the bowl of a food processor fitted with the steel blade. Process until smooth.

5. With the machine running, pour the simmering milk through the processor tube. It will come together into a smooth mixture.

6. Fill the espresso cups three-quarters full.

7. Place the espresso cups into the brownie pan.

8. After you've placed the brownie pan in the oven, carefully pour the boiling water into the pan three-quarters of the way up the sides of the espresso cups.

9. Bake for about 15 minutes, or until the sides are firm but a dime-sized area in the center of each cup is still jiggly.

10. Remove the espresso cups from the pan, and let sit for about 15 minutes before serving or chill completely.

> **BROWNIE POINTER**
>
> I like serving these warm with a chilled, flavored syrup: Mix ½ cup (100 g) sugar with ½ cup (125 mL) water and bring to a boil. Boil until slightly thickened, about 5 minutes. Add any of the following:
>
> • 2 Tbsp (30 mL) freshly chopped mint
>
> • 2 Tbsp (30 mL) freshly chopped ginger, alone or with peeled, diced pears
>
> • 2 Tbsp (30 mL) of your favorite liqueur, cherry and coffee being especially good
>
> Let the mixture steep. Chill the syrup before drizzling on top of the pots.

CHAPTER 6
Icy, Hot, Fruity, Fudgy Brownie Desserts

FROZEN HOT CHOCOLATE

YIELD: 3 CUPS (750 ML)

There's an ice cream company in my hometown that produces a wonderful zero butterfat chocolate ice "cream." One day, as I licked spoonful after spoonful from the container, I read the ingredients and decided that I could make it myself, perhaps not with its shelf-life stabilizers, but with a long enough shelf life to allow my husband and me to eat the entire batch in less than a week. I call it Frozen Hot Chocolate because it has the chocolaty richness of the drink but is bracingly cold. Don't serve it stone hard. Allow it to soften a bit or serve it right out of the ice cream freezer if you have one. And don't miss the additional Brownie Pointers at the end of the recipe.

1 cup (200 g) sugar

½ cup (55 g) cocoa

1½ cups (375 mL) water

½ cup (125 mL) skim milk

½ cup (125 mL) strong, brewed coffee

1 Tbsp (15 mL) good-quality whisky (optional)

pinch kosher salt

1. Place all the ingredients in a large saucepan.

2. Bring to a gentle simmer and stir until all the sugar is dissolved.

3. Simmer for about 15 minutes or until slightly reduced.

4. Pour into a bowl and refrigerate until cold.

5. Place in an ice cream machine and freeze according to the manufacturer's instructions, or pour into two 9-inch (23 cm) square containers and store in the freezer. Every half-hour or so, use a fork to stir it up so it becomes slushy.

6. If you have frozen it solid, let it sit in the fridge for about 10 minutes or on the counter for about 5 minutes before serving to soften it enough to scoop. Or place chunks of it in the food processor and pulse until just smooth.

BROWNIE POINTERS

- This makes a wonderfully rich smoothie. Place 2 scoops into a blender with a ripe banana or some ripe raspberries. Blend just enough to purée the fruit without melting the ice.

- This recipe also makes easy frozen fudge pops. Pour the cooled chocolate mixture into pop molds and freeze for about 3 hours, until firm.

SCHRAFFT'S NUTTY HOT FUDGE/ BUTTERSCOTCH SUNDAE

YIELD: 4 SERVINGS

Schrafft's restaurants no longer exist in New York City, alas. My wonderful Grandma Mae used to take me there after the movies for either a butterscotch or hot fudge sundae. To this day, I can never decide which I prefer, so I combined them and, next to a brownie, this is my favorite dessert. The key here is the temperature—the ice cream just beginning to melt on the outside so it would fall off a cone if it were on one; the hot fudge and butterscotch sauces warm and hardening as they come into contact with the ice cream but not so hot as to liquefy the ice cream all at once. You must have a cold core. Then the nuts: lightly salted so the salt adheres but doesn't overpower the sauces. And then, of course, there's the company you devour this with. No one is allowed to mention calories, guilt or any other passion-palling topic.

8 scoops vanilla ice cream

1 cup (250 mL) Chocolate Fudge Sauce (see page 19)

1 cup (250 mL) Caramel Butterscotch Sauce (see page 18)

½ cup (125 mL) Mixed Salted Nuts (see page 20)

BROWNIE POINTER

Coffee ice cream can also be used and is delicious.

---

1. Have 4 martini glasses ready.

2. Thirty minutes prior to serving, remove the ice cream from the freezer and soften in the fridge.

3. Ten minutes prior to serving, place the Chocolate Fudge and Caramel Butterscotch sauces, if they are cold, over a pot of simmering water to soften up.

4. Pour about 2 Tbsp (30 mL) chocolate sauce in the bottom of each glass.

5. Top with a scoop of ice cream.

6. Drizzle with caramel sauce.

7. Top with a second scoop of ice cream. Drizzle with both sauces.

8. Sprinkle with nuts.

Chocolate Eggnog Tart

YIELD: 10–12 SERVINGS

My friend Selby recently reached into her office fridge and pulled out a container of eggnog left over from the previous weekend's Christmas party. On this particular day, I'd planned to bake a chocolate curd tart, but a lightbulb went on in my head: why not make a chocolate eggnog tart instead? Here's the result. Thanks, Sel, for the inspiration.

one 10-inch (25 cm) prebaked Pâte Sucrée au Chocolat tart shell (see page 5)

9 oz (255 g) bittersweet chocolate, chopped

1 oz (28 g) unsweetened chocolate, chopped

2 cups (500 mL) eggnog

2½ cups (625 mL) whipping cream, divided

2 Tbsp (30 mL) rum

½ tsp (2 mL) freshly grated nutmeg

2 eggs

¼ cup (30 g) icing sugar

2 Tbsp (30 mL) rum

ground chocolate for garnish

freshly ground nutmeg for garnish

1. Preheat the oven to 300°F (150°C). Have the tart shell ready.

2. Place both chopped chocolates in a medium-sized bowl.

3. In a medium pan, over medium heat, bring the eggnog and ½ cup (125 mL) of the cream to just below the boil.

4. Pour over the chocolate in the bowl. Let sit for 5 minutes.

5. Gently whisk the cream into the chocolate until completely mixed.

6. Add the rum and nutmeg.

7. Whisk together the eggs and gradually whisk them into the warm chocolate until thick and glossy, about 1 minute. Pour into a pitcher for easy pouring into the tart shell.

8. Place the tart shell on rack in the oven. Pour the chocolate mixture into the shell.

9. Bake for about 30 minutes or until the filling is barely set. It should still jiggle slightly in the center.

10. Whip the remaining 2 cups (500 mL) cream with the icing sugar and rum. Serve each slice with a dollop of whipped cream dusted with chocolate and nutmeg.

FRUIT CHOCOLATE CRUMBLES:
PEAR, CHERRY, CRANBERRY, RASPBERRY

YIELD: 6 SERVINGS

This is the easiest and most delicious fruit dessert. You'll make this so often that soon you won't even need the recipe. In fact, I'm not really going to give you one because, depending upon the fruit, you may need more or less sugar and cornstarch. Just follow my guidelines and you'll have guaranteed success. Serve warm with vanilla ice cream, crème fraîche or Crème Anglaise (page 15).

4 cups (1 L) fruit: raspberries, cranberries, peeled and diced pears, pitted sweet or sour cherries, or any combination of these fruits

brown sugar to taste (see instructions)

lemon or other juice, water or liqueur to taste (see instructions)

cornstarch (see instructions)

spices: cinnamon, ginger, nutmeg (see instructions)

1 recipe Rich Chocolate Crumble (see page 11)

icing sugar for dusting

BROWNIE POINTER

This is a great brunch recipe, too. The night before, prepare the berry mixture and place in the baking pan. Prepare the crumble but keep it separate. Put both in the fridge. Just before baking, toss the berries to redistribute the juices. Top with crumble and bake as directed.

---

1. Preheat the oven to 350°F (180°C). Butter a 9-inch (23 cm) square or round glass baking dish with 2-inch (5 cm) sides.

2. Place the fruit in a bowl. Start by sprinkling with ¼ cup (50 g) sugar. Let sit for about 15 minutes. Taste the juice at the bottom of the bowl. Is it too sweet? Squeeze in some fresh lemon juice. Is it not sweet enough? Add some more sugar.

3. If your fruit hasn't given off any liquid after sitting in the sugar, add any one of the suggested liquids in the ingredient list. Cherries might not give up juice, cranberries won't, and if your pears aren't ripe, they won't either. Start with ¼ cup (60 mL) of fruit juice: orange, cranberry or even apple. Use just enough to dissolve the cornstarch. You can use liqueur, too, if you want: framboise with raspberries or Poire William with pears are fabulous.

4. Sprinkle 1 Tbsp (15 mL) cornstarch over the fruit and toss to make sure it gets thoroughly moistened by the fruit juice. Fruits that are naturally high in pectin, like cranberries, may not need this at all, but if you like your crumbles more like pie filling, then add another teaspoon or two (5–10 mL) of cornstarch dissolved in some of the liquid. Let sit for a few minutes and toss the fruit together again.

5. Add some spices to taste. Try ginger (1 tsp/5 mL) and/or nutmeg (¼ tsp/1 mL) with pears. Cinnamon is great with cranberries (1 tsp/5 mL); I don't think you need anything with raspberries but a bit of almond extract (up to 1 tsp/5 mL) is good with both kinds of cherries (try ¼ tsp/1 mL at first).

6. Tumble the entire mixture into the prepared pan, including all accumulated liquid, dissolved sugar and cornstarch and spices.

7. Top with the crumble and bake until you see the liquid bubbling around the edges and up through the center of the crumble. If it's not bubbling, the cornstarch won't thicken and you will have a grainy sauce. The crumble will be crisp and firm when done. If crumble starts to darken before the juices come to a boil, cover with aluminum foil to prevent burning.

8. Before serving, dust the top with icing sugar.

FRESH BERRIES WITH CHOCOLATE AND CORNMEAL CRUMBLE

YIELD: 6 SERVINGS

In the midst of winter, there was a sale on blueberries and raspberries. The berries were plump and flavorful, an amazing feat in January. What an inspiration! But as much as I love really good fresh fruit, I love really crunchy crumble more than anything else, which is why people who know me well know that when I am at a loss for what to make, crumble it is. Usually, though, it's with fruit that's been frozen or somewhat over the hill, since crumble hides a multitude of sins (soft fruit, loss of great blush) while simultaneously releasing a myriad of hidden flavors and abundant sugars. In this case, however, the fruit needed no such help. It could have been served fresh, but could also have benefited from a helping of delicious toasted almonds tossed with crispy bits and shards of chocolate. It was a revelation. The Italians call the cornmeal crumble (served without fruit) sbrisolona, *but no recipe that I've ever seen calls for chocolate!*

Fruit Salad:

1 pint (150 g) blueberries

1 pint (150 g) raspberries

1 Tbsp (15 mL) sugar

1 Tbsp (15 mL) lemon juice (from about half a lemon) or your favorite liqueur

1. Toss all the ingredients together.

2. Set aside to steep for an hour.

Crumble:

1 egg yolk

1 tsp (5 mL) almond extract

1 tsp (5 mL) vanilla extract

3½ oz (100 g) 70% chocolate

4¼ oz (120 g) raw almonds, whole

1 cup + 2 Tbsp (145 g) all-purpose flour

6 Tbsp (90 g) cornmeal

1. Preheat the oven to 350°F (180°C). Grease an 8-inch (20 cm) springform pan.

2. In a small bowl, whisk together the egg yolk and extracts.

3. Chop the chocolate into pieces half the size of chocolate chips.

4. Place the almonds in a roasting pan and bake until fragrant and toasted, about 10 minutes.

5. While the almonds are toasting, mix together the flour, cornmeal, sugar and salt.

¾ cup (150 g) sugar

½ tsp (2 mL) kosher salt

1 cup *less* 2 Tbsp (200 g) cold butter

icing sugar for dusting

6. Remove the almonds from the oven and cool. Coarsely chop and add to the flour mixture. Toss to mix.

7. Cut the butter into small cubes and toss with the flour mixture.

8. Using your hands, rub the butter cubes between your thumb and forefinger, pressing them flat or into smaller pieces.

9. When you have a bowl of pea-sized crumbs, drizzle the egg yolk mixture over the crumbs. Toss lightly with your hands.

10. Rub the mixture using your palms to moisten the crumbs evenly and to pick up the floury stuff at the bottom of the bowl.

11. Add the chopped chocolate and crumble it through the crumbs.

12. Pour the crumbs into the 8-inch (20 cm) pan. Lightly press it into the pan, leaving the top uneven and crumbly looking.

13. Bake for about 20–30 minutes, until the top is golden brown. Don't worry if it's not firm when you remove it from the oven. It will firm up as it cools.

14. Cool completely in the pan.

15. Toss the steeped berries and spoon onto a plate. Remove the springform ring and break up the crumble into rough pieces. Sprinkle these pieces on top of the berries and dust with icing sugar.

16. Vanilla ice cream wouldn't hurt either!

PEAR GINGER CRUMBLE

YIELD: 6 SERVINGS

The whole family was coming over for dinner. There was some crumble lingering in the freezer and an article about pears that caught my eye. Putting the two together was easy, but how to make it special? Add some cocoa, Armagnac and candied ginger, that's how. Serve with chilled yogurt.

6 ripe pears, unpeeled, cored and cut into 1-inch (2.5 cm) dice

1 Tbsp (15 mL) cornstarch

1 Tbsp (15 mL) cocoa

1 tsp (5 mL) cinnamon

pinch kosher salt

1 Tbsp (15 mL) lemon juice

1 Tbsp (15 mL) Armagnac

1 Tbsp (15 mL) candied ginger, finely diced

2 cups (500 mL) Rich Chocolate Crumble (see page 11)

1. Preheat the oven to 400°F (200°C).

2. Toss together the cornstarch, cocoa, cinnamon, salt, lemon juice and Armagnac with the pears until the pears are well coated. Let sit for about 10 minutes. Add the candied ginger and toss well.

3. Pour into a 9-inch (23 cm) square casserole dish or baking pan, making sure to scrape in all the juices.

4. Top with the crumble.

5. Bake for 40 minutes or until the juices are bubbling.

6. Remove from the oven and serve warm.

> **BROWNIE POINTER**
>
> The easiest way to slice pears (and apples) is to slice down from the stem along the edge of what you imagine to be the core. You will have a side of the fruit. Turn the cut fruit onto the flat side on a cutting board and slice off another piece and so on until you have sliced around the core. No need to use a corer. Nibble around the core or throw into vegetable stock (it adds a nice sweetness) or when you are making applesauce or pear purée. Proceed to slice the pears (or apples) thinly into even pieces or chunks.

CRANBERRY GANACHE CRUMBLE FLAN
(AKA JOHN'S BIRTHDAY TART)

YIELD: 6–8 SERVINGS

I used to make a variation of this flan at The Original Bakery Café but we always had problems with the berries: sometimes they'd cook and sometimes they wouldn't because we'd mound the crumble on top of them, creating insulation from the heat of the oven. Despite this, one ardent fan would purchase it for his birthday every year and even called me up at home, after the store closed, begging me to make it for him—which I did, of course. When I went on to do other things, we lost touch. Imagine my amazement when he recently called me at work to order "his" tart once again. How he found me, I don't know. Here's an updated version of John's Birthday Tart. You can make this in any kind of tart shell, from 8–9 inches (20–23 cm) or even in a square or rectangular version. It's helpful if the pan has a removable bottom. You may also substitute the Rich Chocolate Crumble (page 11) for the crumble used here.

¼ recipe Pâte Sucrée (see page 3)

Crust:

1. Preheat the oven to 350°F (180°C).

2. On a lightly floured surface, roll out the pastry dough to slightly less than ¼ inch (5 mm) thick and about 12 inches (30 cm) in diameter, or at least 2 inches (5 cm) more than the size of your baking pan.

3. Fold it in half gently, lift it with your hands and place the folded side in the middle of a 9-inch (23 cm) fluted flan shell with a removable bottom. Unfold the dough.

4. Gently press the dough down into the flan shell, being sure that it fits snugly into the bottom and up the sides. Make sure there is an even amount of dough around the sides. Cut off any excess dough from the top. Prick the bottom with a fork.

5. Chill for about 30 minutes or until firm.

6. Remove from the fridge and line the pastry with foil. Fill the foil with beans or weights to help the dough hold shape while it's baking.

7. Bake for 12 minutes. Remove the foil and weights and return the flan shell to the oven. Bake for an additional 5–8 minutes, or until the shell is golden brown.

8. Remove from the oven and cool on a rack.

continued on page 179 ...

Cranberry Ganache Crumble Flan (continued)

Crumble:

3 cups (750 mL) chocolate brownie or chocolate cake crumbs

2 Tbsp (30 mL) sugar

1 tsp (1 mL) ground cinnamon

½ tsp (2 mL) kosher salt

3–4 Tbsp (45–55 mL) butter, melted

1. Mix all the ingredients together in a medium-sized bowl, adding only enough butter to create a moist but not sodden crumble.

2. Squeeze the crumbs together; some pieces should be about the size of peas.

Filling:

1 lb (454 g) fresh or frozen cranberries, divided

¾ cup (150 g) sugar

1 Tbsp (15 mL) cornstarch

2 Tbsp (30 mL) water or raspberry liqueur

½ tsp (2 mL) ground cinnamon

⅛ tsp (0.5 mL) kosher salt

2 cups (500 mL) ganache (see page 13)

icing sugar for dusting

1. Preheat the oven to 350°F (180°C).

2. Place half the cranberries, and the sugar, cornstarch, water, cinnamon and salt into a medium-sized saucepan. Stir to combine.

3. Place the pot over low heat and stir to dissolve the sugar and cornstarch. Increase the heat slightly and cook for about 5–8 minutes, stirring occasionally. As the mixture cooks, the cranberries will begin to release their juices.

4. When the filling comes to a boil, stir gently for about 3 minutes. The cornstarch will thicken the juice and it will become clear. Remove from the heat. The mixture should be lumpy with fruit in a shiny, thickened sauce.

5. Add the reserved cranberries and mix well. Cool for about 10 minutes.

6. Spread the ganache evenly over the bottom of the prepared crust.

7. Give the filling one last stir before pouring it over the ganache. Spread evenly.

8. Distribute the prepared crumble over the fruit.

9. Bake for 20 minutes, or until the crumble is firm and you see the filling bubbling at the edges of the flan.

10. Remove from the oven and serve warm, dusted with icing sugar and accompanied by vanilla ice cream.

BROWNIE POINTER

A wonderful variation is to reduce the cranberries by one-third and replace them with 2 pints (300 g) of fresh or frozen raspberries, adding them in place of the second addition of cranberries.

Rum Raisin Brownie Pie

YIELD: 8–10 SERVINGS

The more I bake with chocolate, the more convinced I am that the bitterer the better and the lower the temperature the better. All work to conserve and to enhance the rich, indescribable and multitudinous flavors and aromas of chocolate. Coax chocolate, don't bully it.

1 cup (120 g) big, plump raisins

¼ cup (60 mL) rum

1 cup (227 g) butter

¾ cup (165 g) brown sugar

1 cup *less* 2 Tbsp (175 g) granulated sugar

7 oz (200 g) bitter chocolate, chopped

3½ oz (100 g) 85% bittersweet chocolate, chopped

5 eggs

1 tsp (5 mL) vanilla extract

1 cup (130 g) instant flour (see page vi) or all-purpose flour

1 tsp (5 mL) kosher salt

1. Preheat the oven to 350°F (180°C). Grease a 10-inch (25 cm) pie plate with vegetable spray.

2. Place the raisins and rum in a small saucepan over medium heat. Bring to a boil. Turn off the heat and set aside.

3. Melt the butter in a saucepan over medium heat.

4. Add the brown and white sugars and stir until it becomes a single, thick mass.

5. Add the chopped chocolates and stir. Let sit until completely melted. Stir again until smooth.

6. Add the eggs and mix until smooth.

7. Add the vanilla.

8. Add the flour and salt and mix until completely smooth and glossy.

9. Stir in the rum and raisins. Stir to blend completely.

10. Pour into the pie pan: It will completely fill the pie plate but this is okay since it won't rise much.

11. Bake 25 minutes, or until the edges are set but the center is still soft.

12. Remove from the oven and let rest about 30 minutes. Serve warm with vanilla ice cream. Amazing.

Brownie Ice Cream Cake

YIELD: 12 SLICES

If the truth be known, this yummy cake came about when I neglected to read a brownie recipe properly. Rather than chuck it, I used it for an ice cream cake—this is the result. I decided that this could only be better with a better brownie to begin with. It's got just about everything: hot, cold, soft, crunchy, sweet and salty. Best of all it's quick to assemble and amazing to eat.

½ recipe any baked brownies (about 3 cups/750 mL chopped)

½ cup (85 g) peanut butter chips

3 oz (85 g) bittersweet chocolate, chopped

1 cup (250 mL) Mocha-ed Nuts (see page 21)

2 pints (1 L) vanilla ice cream, softened slightly

1 cup (250 mL) Caramel Butterscotch Sauce (see page 18)

pinch kosher salt

1. Have a 10-inch (28 cm) springform pan ready. Line the bottom with parchment paper.

2. Roughly chop the brownies into 1-inch (2.5 cm) pieces and place in a bowl with the peanut butter chips and chopped chocolate.

3. Roughly chop half the pecans and add to the bowl. Toss to mix the ingredients.

4. Scoop the ice cream into the bowl and mash in all the ingredients, using a rubber spatula. Mix thoroughly. Unless it's really hot in your kitchen, the ice cream won't melt in the less than 5 minutes that it takes to assemble this cake.

5. Scoop the mixture into the prepared pan, and spread as evenly as possible. Freeze for about 30 minutes.

6. When ready to serve, wet a kitchen towel with hot water and press against the sides of the pan. You will see the ice cream melt at the edges. Remove the sides of the springform.

7. Slide the cake onto a serving plate.

8. Drizzle with the Caramel Butterscotch Sauce and sprinkle with the pinch of kosher salt and the remaining nuts. Slice in wedges and serve each plate drizzled with caramel sauce.

Peanut Butter Caramel Tart

YIELD: 10 SERVINGS

Oh yes, another chocolate and peanut butter recipe! I just can't help it. This is a quick and easy tart to assemble. It freezes beautifully and pleases just about everyone.

½ recipe Pâte Sucrée au Chocolat (see page 5)

½ cup (125 mL) Caramel Butterscotch Sauce (see page 18), cooled

½ cup (60 g) coarsely chopped peanuts

½ cup (100 g) sugar

5 Tbsp (70 mL) peanut butter at room temperature

5 Tbsp (70 g) butter at room temperature

5 Tbsp (70 g) cream cheese at room temperature

½ cup + 1 Tbsp (70 g) icing sugar, sifted

2 oz (56 g) bittersweet chocolate, melted (see page vii for tips)

1 cup (250 mL) Shiny Chocolate Glaze (see page 2)

1. Preheat the oven to 350°F (180°C).

2. Roll the Pâte Sucrée au Chocolat to a circle about 9 inches (23 cm) in diameter.

3. Press it into the bottom and sides of a 7½-inch (19 cm) fluted tart pan with a removable bottom. Trim any excess dough to make the top edge neat and the sides even. Wrap and freeze the scraps for another use.

4. Prick the bottom of the dough with a fork. Line with foil flush with the sides and bottom and weight with dried beans or lentils.

5. Bake for 15 minutes and remove the foil carefully. Touch the center to see if it is fully baked. If it is firm, remove from the oven. If it still feels soft and moist, bake for an additional 5 minutes.

6. Cool.

7. Spread the Caramel Butterscotch Sauce in the cooled chocolate shell. Place in the freezer.

8. Place the chopped peanuts on a piece of parchment paper or oiled foil. Keep them in a small circle about 4 inches (10 cm) in diameter.

9. Place the ½ cup (100 g) sugar in a small saucepan. Add 1 Tbsp (15 mL) cold water and bring to a boil.

10. Boil until the water evaporates and the sugar caramelizes into a rich golden brown.

11. Immediately pour over the nuts. Allow the praline to harden completely.

12. In the bowl of an electric mixer, beat together the peanut butter, butter and cream cheese until smooth and fluffy.

13. Add the icing sugar and continue to beat until light and fluffy. Add the melted chocolate and mix to blend, scraping the sides of the bowl. Set aside.

14. Gently warm the chocolate glaze over a pan of simmering water. It should be just warm enough to pour.

continued on page 186 . . .

Banana Walnut Caramel Crunch Chocolate Pie

YIELD: ONE 10-INCH (28 CM) FLAN, ABOUT 15 SLENDER BUT RICH SERVINGS

Hold the presses! I just created this for my niece Maya's seventeenth birthday and got such an incredible reaction that I had to include it in the book. Oozy, crunchy, chocolaty, it's best served warm. Chilled is fine, too, although room temperature is better. You can make it a day ahead and chill it, unglazed, then finish it with ganache shortly before serving.

¼ recipe Pâte Sucrée (see page 3)

2 Tbsp (30 mL) butter

¼ cup (55 g) brown sugar

½ tsp (2 mL) ground cinnamon

4 ripe bananas

1 cup (120 g) walnut pieces, toasted, coarsely chopped

1 cup (250 mL) Caramel Butterscotch Sauce (see page 18)

1–2 Tbsp (15–30 mL) rum or water

1½ cups (375 mL) ganache (see page 13)

whipped cream (optional)

1. Roll out the dough to ⅛-inch (3 mm) thickness. Press into a 10-inch (28 cm) round, fluted flan pan with a removable bottom. Trim excess dough to make the edges neat. Chill for at least 30 minutes.

2. Preheat the oven to 350°F (180°C).

3. Prick the bottom of the shell with a fork. Line with foil and weight with dried beans or lentils.

4. Bake for ¹2 minutes until set. Remove the foil and weights and bake until golden brown.

5. Cool completely.

6. In a large sauté pan, preferably nonstick, melt the butter until bubbly.

7. Add the brown sugar and stir until the sugar and butter have turned to caramel, about 5 minutes. Add the cinnamon and blend well.

8. Slice the bananas horizontally in half. If they break into smaller pieces, don't worry.

9. Place them flat side down in the Caramel Butterscotch Sauce and sauté until golden on 1 side, about 3 minutes, and then gently flip them over, coating the rounded side with sauce. Cook for 1 minute longer.

10. Remove the bananas from the pan and place flat side down in the tart shell, distributing them evenly.

11. Sprinkle with half the toasted walnuts.

12. Pour the caramel sauce into the sauté pan with the banana caramel and bring to a low simmer.

13. Add the rum and boil for 1 minute. Remove from the heat and let cool for about 15 minutes.

14. Pour the caramel mixture over the bananas and walnuts, tilting the pan to spread it evenly.

15. Place in the fridge to cool for at least half an hour before glazing with the ganache.

16. About 30 minutes prior to serving, remove from the fridge.

17. Warm the ganache just enough for it to pour, either in the microwave on medium power or in a bowl over barely simmering water to between 80–85°F (27–30°C).

18. Pour over the caramel, tilting the pan so that the ganache covers everything. It should be even with no bumps showing.

19. Chop the remaining walnuts to a medium-fine consistency and sprinkle them either all over the top or just around the edges.

20. Serve with whipped cream.

Medjool Dates Stuffed with Brownie Curd and Crème Fraîche

YIELD: 8 STUFFED DATES

A few years ago, my husband, Howard, and our kids, Joanna and Alexander, drove through Napa Valley. We stopped at a gourmet store and picked up a picnic lunch, which, among other things, consisted of French prunes stuffed with foie gras. We then sat in an olive arbor overlooking a spectacular vineyard while we stuffed our faces with the most incredible prunes we'd ever eaten. This particular scene came to mind when I spotted some big, moist Medjool dates in the produce department. Having just concocted Brownie Curd, it was on my mind to do something original with it, so stuffing the curd, which has the smooth unctuousness of foie gras, into the date wasn't so far-fetched. Unlike prunes, which have a slight tartness to them, dates are really sweet, so I needed something to mediate between the richness of the date and that of the curd. I chose crème fraîche, and wow! While these can be devoured at room temperature, the flavor really shines when slightly warmed in the oven.

2 oz (56 g) walnuts, toasted and finely chopped

8 Medjool dates

3 Tbsp (45 mL) crème fraîche

3 Tbsp (45 mL) Brownie Curd (see page 8)

1 orange, grated rind of

1. Preheat the oven to 300°F (150°C).

2. Place the ground walnuts on a plate.

3. Slice the dates open just enough to remove the pit. Do not halve.

4. Gently spread open the sides and press down the interior flesh to make some room for the fillings.

5. Using a small spoon, divide the crème fraîche among the 8 dates.

6. Do the same with the Brownie Curd, covering the crème fraîche.

7. Gently squeeze the sides of the dates towards the center to contain the filling.

8. Zest the orange over the dates so that a few strands of rind fall evenly on top.

◄ Chocolate Sandwich Cookies, made with Pâte Sucrée au Chocolat (page 5), Medjool Dates Stuffed with Brownie Curd and Crème Fraîche (this page), Brownie Truffles (page 193)

continued on next page . . .

9. Holding the dates by their sides, dip them into the ground walnuts so the top is completely covered.

10. Place the dates on a cookie sheet and warm in the oven for no more than 3–4 minutes, before the chocolate fully melts but enough to warm the crème fraîche.

11. Serve immediately.

BROWNIE POINTER

Having run the Specialty Department at the Toronto Whole Foods Market for a while, I was constantly looking for, and finding, new cheese combinations. One of the most unusual, and one that people either loved or hated, was a Portuguese chocolate "salami" with Gorgonzola cheese. This is definitely a variation on the cheese course, and can substitute for dessert.

Follow the instructions, substituting crumbled Gorgonzola, or your favorite tangy blue cheese, for the crème fraîche. Proceed as per the recipe. What a zinger of a combination! Sweet, salty, protein, fat and fiber . . . just about everything you need for a balanced diet!

BROWNIE TRUFFLES

YIELD: IT DEPENDS . . .

I watch TV while I bake, which may explain my propensity for leaving out ingredients. Who can measure accurately or at all when a crucial and sexy female character is said to possess a body part usually associated with a man (honest, Ally McBeal, November 5, 2000)? So it was fortunate that this recipe required no measuring at all, just mixing and adding ingredients, some of which were results of my inattention. These aren't your standard truffles but they're quick and easy to make, and they make good use of leftovers and scraps.

2 cups (500 mL) brownie or chocolate cake scraps

½ cup (60 g) Rummed Raisins (or Rummed Dried Fruit) (see page 24)

½ cup (60 g) chopped nuts (optional)

2–4 Tbsp (30–60 mL) your favorite liqueur, or rum if using Rummed Raisins, or brewed coffee

1 cup (250 mL) ganache (see page 13)

cocoa for rolling

BROWNIE POINTER

Roll these truffles in chopped walnuts or almonds instead of the cocoa.

---

1. Place the brownie scraps, raisins and nuts, if using, in the bowl of a food processor.

2. Pulse briefly to mix everything but not long enough to turn it to mush, about 3 or 4 times.

3. Add the liqueur a tablespoon at a time and pulse once or twice to blend. The mixture should be barely moist enough to hold together but not mushy or wet.

4. Scrape into a bowl with a rubber spatula and refrigerate for 30 minutes.

5. Remove the mixture from the fridge and use a small scoop or teaspoon to make small balls the size of a truffle.

6. Roll between your hands to make them uniform in shape. Refrigerate for 30 minutes.

7. Barely warm the ganache. Line a baking tray with parchment paper.

8. Place a truffle on a fork and dip completely into the ganache, allowing the excess chocolate to drip through the tines and back into the bowl.

9. Use the tip of a knife to nudge the truffle off the fork and onto the parchment-lined tray. Repeat with the remaining truffles.

10. Refrigerate until the ganache is set, about 1 hour.

11. Place the cocoa in a bowl and roll each truffle in the cocoa. Place on a serving plate or in a small petit four cup for after dinner service.

12. Store in the fridge. Or freeze them and serve frozen. Amazing.

MICHELLE'S BIRTHDAY CRUMBLE

YIELD: 10 SERVINGS

My colleague Michelle liked the crumbs on top of my Chocolate Brownie Crumb Cake (page 85) so much that she asked if I could make her a birthday cake that was all crumbs. Yes, there's something intensely satisfying about the crunch and crumble of crumbs. Here are two versions, one to use up old cake or cookie crumbs, the other from scratch. Both are ridiculously easy to make. Depending upon the kinds of crumbs you use in v.1, you will get something different every time—and that's a good thing. It staves off culinary boredom. However, if you want the same thing over and over again because it's simply too good, use v.2. The end result is a slightly moist, rich layer underneath and a gloriously crisp and crunchy layer on top.

Michelle's Birthday Crumble v.1

2 cups (500 mL) chocolate cake and/or cookie crumbs

¾ cup (150 g) + 1 Tbsp (15 mL) sugar

¾ cup (100 g) whole wheat or multigrain flour

2 oz (56 g) ground toasted almonds, walnuts or pecans (optional)

1 tsp (5 mL) cinnamon (optional)

⅛ tsp (0.5 mL) nutmeg

¼ cup (60 mL) melted butter, or enough to allow the crumbs to just hold their shape

2 egg whites

¼ tsp (2 mL) kosher salt

3 oz (85 g) chocolate chips

¼ cup (65 mL) ganache (see page 13), warmed

icing sugar for dusting

1. Preheat the oven to 350°F (180°C). Spray a 9-inch (23 cm) tart pan with a removable bottom with vegetable spray.

2. Place the crumbs into a medium-sized bowl.

3. Add the ¾ cup (150 g) of sugar and flour, and nuts and cinnamon, if using (see Brownie Pointers).

4. Mix until blended.

5. Add the melted butter and mix until all the crumbs are coated.

6. Squeeze some crumbs in the palm of your hand. They should just barely hold together. If they don't, dribble in a few more drops of melted butter until they do.

7. Whisk the egg whites either by hand or with an electric mixer (although I use an immersion blender to do this job) until they are frothy. Add the salt and the 1 Tbsp (15 mL) sugar. Mix until the whites are thick and white. They don't have to form peaks (but it's okay if they do).

8. Fold into the crumbs.

9. Press half the crumbs into the prepared pan. Fold the chocolate chips into the remaining crumbs.

10. Top the pan with the remaining crumbs by squeezing them into your hand and then breaking them into big lumps. Cover the top evenly.

11. Bake for 30 minutes.

12. Cool completely to make sure the crumble is crisp. Carefully remove the outer ring of the tart pan, then drizzle the crumble with the ganache or dust with icing sugar. Or both: Allow the drizzled ganache to dry and then lightly sift with icing sugar.

Michelle's Birthday Crumble v.2

¼ cup + 1 Tbsp (70 g) brown sugar

¾ cup (150 g) granulated sugar, divided

½ cup (65 g) multigrain or whole wheat flour

¼ cup (30 g) cocoa

¼ tsp (2 mL) cinnamon

¼ tsp (2 mL) espresso powder

¼ tsp (2 mL) kosher salt

⅛ tsp (1 mL) nutmeg

½ cup (125 mL) melted butter, cooled

8 oz (227 g) toasted, coarsely chopped almonds

6¼ oz (175 g) 70% bittersweet chocolate, chopped into the size of chocolate chips

2 egg whites

¼ cup (60 mL) ganache (see page 13)

icing sugar for dusting

1. Preheat the oven to 350°F (180°C). Line a 9-inch (23 cm) round springform pan with parchment paper. Spray the sides and paper with vegetable spray.

2. Place the brown sugar in a bowl. Scale the white sugar and remove 1 Tbsp (15 mL) to mix with the egg whites. Add the remaining granulated sugar, the flour, cocoa, cinnamon, espresso powder, salt and nutmeg to the bowl.

3. Pour in the cooled melted butter and mix lightly to coat the crumbs. (They will clump together when squeezed.)

4. Add the nuts and chocolate and mix to incorporate.

5. Beat the egg whites until frothy and add the remaining 1 Tbsp (15 mL) sugar. Beat until they are no longer the color of eggs whites, but instead light and pure white.

6. Fold into the crumb mixture.

7. Gently pat half the crumbs into the prepared pan. Don't press hard—just make an even layer with no holes.

8. Drop the remaining crumbs evenly over the top in blobs the size of marbles. Press them gently to stick to the bottom layer.

9. Bake for about 30 minutes. The crumbs will still feel soft to the touch but will firm up as they cool. Don't overbake.

10. Cool. Remove from the pan by opening the ring and sliding a broad metal spatula beneath the crumble. Transfer onto a plate. Drizzle with the ganache (warmed) and let it set before dusting with icing sugar.

BROWNIE POINTERS

- For v.1, if the crumbs you are using contain cinnamon, you can leave it out. But if the crumbs don't have any nuts, you should add them.

- V.1 can be made in a cake pan as well. A springform is the best alternative to the tart shell, but a parchment-lined cake pan will work, too. Just make sure the crumble is chilled before turning it over onto a plate. Remove the parchment, place another plate on the top and flip over so it's right side up again.

MIDNIGHT BROWNIE TART WITH CHERRY COMPOTE

YIELD: 10 PIECES

These are dark, incredibly rich and delicious because I've used a high percentage chocolate without increasing the sugar. They are very gooey at the center but that's as they should be. They're made in a tart pan only because sometimes you need to be reminded that brownies are very adaptable, and shaping them as a tart suggests that they be served with something else . . . like the cherry compote. When I made this the first time, my plan was to round out the flavors with crème fraîche, vanilla ice cream or even custard sauce, but I didn't have any. However, after tasting the brownie and the compote together, I realized I didn't need to gild the lily . . . or in this case the brownie. The compote is also delicious over ice cream, pancakes, rice pudding, etc.

9 oz (255 g) 70–80% chocolate

1 cup (227 g) butter

1⅓ cups (265 g) sugar

5 eggs

1 tsp (5 mL) vanilla extract

2 Tbsp (30 mL) instant flour (see page vi) or all-purpose flour

½ tsp (2 mL) cinnamon

½ tsp (2 mL) instant espresso powder

¼ tsp (1 mL) kosher salt

1 recipe Cherry Compote

1. Preheat the oven to 300°F (150°C). Spray an 8-inch (20 cm) fluted tart pan with a removable bottom with vegetable spray.

2. Chop the chocolate and melt in a bowl over simmering water.

3. Melt the butter in a saucepan and add the sugar. Whisk until thick and smooth.

4. Add the melted chocolate and remove from the heat. Whisk to incorporate the chocolate.

5. One at a time, add the eggs, whisking until the batter is thick and glossy.

6. Add the vanilla and mix lightly.

7. Add the flour, cinnamon, espresso and salt, mixing only enough to incorporate quickly.

8. Pour the batter into the prepared tart pan.

9. Bake for 30 minutes or just until the center is barely puffed. It will still feel jiggly to the touch.

10. Remove from the oven and cool. Serve with Cherry Compote.

Cherry Compote

YIELD: 3 CUPS (750 ML)

1 cup (250 mL) vodka

1 cup (200 g) sugar

1. Place the vodka and sugar in a saucepan and bring to a boil. Reduce the heat and simmer until slightly thickened, about 10 minutes.

continued on page 198 . . .

Midnight Brownie Tart with Cherry Compote (continued)

2 cups (500 mL) fresh, unpitted cherries, washed (if fresh aren't available, use canned cherries, preferably unsweetened)

drops lemon juice

pinch kosher salt

2. Add the cherries, and simmer until soft and the syrup has thickened. The alcohol in the vodka will cook off, so don't worry—you won't get the kids or your guests drunk on brownies with cherries!

3. Remove from the heat and cool. When cool, taste the mixture, and then add drops of lemon juice to balance the sweetness and a tiny pinch of salt to bring out the flavors.

4. Don't forget to warn everyone that there are pits in the cherries and they're there for a reason: the pits enhance the flavor!

5. Store the cherry compote in the fridge.

Index

Page numbers in italics refer to photographs.